Way of the Real Faith
A Choice, a Journey, a Destiny

[VOLUME I OF THE REAL FAITH SERIES]

D. A. Singh, PhD

Elina Publishing

Copyright © 2016 by D. A. Singh

All rights reserved worldwide. No part of this book may be reproduced or transmitted in any form or by any means, electronic or mechanical, including photocopying, scanning, recording, translating into another language, or by any information storage and retrieval system, without written permission from the copyright owner.

Contact information: dasingh@elinapub.com

Unless otherwise indicated, all Scripture quotations are taken from the Holy Bible, New International Version®, NIV®. Copyright ©1973, 1978, 1984, 2011 by Biblica, Inc.™

Used by permission of Zondervan. All rights reserved worldwide. WWW.ZONDERVAN.COM

The "NIV" and "New International Version" are trademarks registered in the United States Patent and Trademark Office by Biblica, Inc.™

Publisher: Elina Publishing, Berrien Springs, Michigan, U.S.A.

http://www.elinapub.com

Cover design: www.elmstreetdesignstudio.net

Way of the Real Faith: A Choice, a Journey, a Destiny/D. A. Singh—1st ed.

ISBN 978-0-9971761-0-0

Ordering information: See page 189.

Contents

About this Book 1
Chapter 1 - Way to the Throne 3
Chapter 2 - Given to Us 13
Chapter 3 - Why He Came 25
Chapter 4 - The Victory 41
Chapter 5 - What Must I Do? 55
Chapter 6 - The New Life 65
Chapter 7 - The Divine Companion 87
Chapter 8 - The Kingdom 95
Chapter 9 - Look! He Comes 105
Chapter 10 - The Enemy 115
Chapter 11 - Two Destinies 131
Chapter 12 - By Faith 141
Chapter 13 - The Book of Books 153
Chapter 14 - News in Advance 167
Chapter 15 - The Signposts 177
Chapter 16 - The New Age 183
Postscript 189
Appendix I—Glossary 191
Appendix II—Books of the Holy Scriptures 195
Index 197

Acknowledgment

The assistance of Allison Singh in reviewing the manuscript and checking the NIV citations is gratefully acknowledged.

Of course, any errors and omissions are the responsibility of the author.

About This Book

Way of the Real Faith: A Choice, a Journey, a Destiny is written for people of all ages, cultures, and backgrounds. The materials are presented in a straightforward and simple way so that even children as young as ten or eleven years old can read and understand the main message. And, of course, this book is for adults too. For many people, this will most likely be the only source to help them understand the one Real Faith that is found in the Holy Scriptures.

As you read this book, you are also introduced to the Holy Scriptures and their core message. The narrative includes Scripture citations in italics, which eliminates the need to constantly turn to external sources. Scripture citations also help those who do not have access to the Holy Scriptures.

This book is not about some religious organization, denomination, doctrine, or creed. Religion and rounds of religious ceremonies do not lead to an understanding of who God is. Hence, for a large number of people, the One God remains unknown and unreachable.

Yet, He has made Himself known. But, people needlessly look for Him in shrines and other places that they have labeled "holy." They try to find Him through books that do not inform them about who He is. They go through rituals hoping to find peace, but the joy and peace they hope for escape them. They continue to search endlessly, but in vain.

The idea of coming to God sounds strange to many people. Yet, He waits with open arms for you to come to Him.

God speaks to people directly through the Holy Scriptures. Hence, this book lets the Sacred Scriptures speak to your mind and heart. The New International Version (2011 edition) has been used herein because it is written in current English, without compromising the meaning of the Hebrew, Aramaic, and Greek languages in which the Scriptures were originally written.

Numbered footnotes are used to explain certain technical terms. You can also look up in the Glossary (Appendix I) the meaning of uncommon words and phrases.

After Scripture citations in italics, references to the Scriptures are given in parentheses, with full names of the books of the Scriptures. The name is not given if a book was already named immediately before a current citation in the same section. Appendix II provides a complete list of the books of the Holy Scriptures.

If you are not familiar with the Holy Scriptures, you may want to read Chapter 13 first.

CHAPTER 1

Way to the Throne

The way to the throne is open, but not many have found it. There is only one way to the throne. It is through the Real Faith. As you read this book, it will be impossible to miss it. The Holy Scriptures point the way to the Real Faith.

> *Let us then approach God's throne of grace with confidence ...* (Hebrews 4:16).

God is the Ruler of the entire universe. *He is the high and exalted One who lives in a high and holy place* (Isaiah 57:15). Many people do not believe that the One who lives in the high and holy place can be approached. But, you can come to Him, and with confidence. You can come to Him, even though it sounds impossible.

Actually, He is waiting for you. But, you must take the first step. You can come before His throne without fear.

In olden days, citizens ruled by a king could come before him. Not anytime; only at certain times when the king held court. Then, too, there had to be a special reason for a person to come before the king. It was mainly to obtain justice or the king's decision to settle disputes. For example, once two women came before King Solomon because each claimed that a newborn child was hers.[1]

The women asked the king to decide whose child the baby was, and to deliver judgment. The women had to come before King Solomon with some preparation. Each had to explain why she thought the child was hers.

Even the queen could not come before the king anytime or for any reason. Often, she had to obtain special permission to come before the king when he was sitting on his throne. Here is the account of Queen Esther coming before King Xerxes[2]:

> *Esther put on her royal robes and stood in the inner court of the palace, in front of the king's hall. The king was sitting on his royal throne in the hall, facing the entrance. When he saw Queen Esther standing in the court, he was pleased with her and held out to her the gold scepter[3] that was in his hand. So Esther approached and touched the tip of the scepter. Then the king asked, "What is it, Queen Esther? What is your request?"* (Esther 5:1–3).

People dressed appropriately when they came before the king. Even Queen Esther put on her royal robes. So, appearing before a king required special decorum (correctness). What if the queen had put on an improper robe? Would the king have still welcomed her?

Today, nations have presidents, prime ministers, and other rulers. But, you cannot simply walk in and meet them. For an ordinary citizen to have an appointment with the president of a country is almost impossible. They are too busy with other things they think are more important than to have a meeting with the common people.

How about the King of the Universe? Can you come before Him at any time?

---

[1] The account is found in 2 Kings 3:16–28.
[2] The name is Ahasuerus in the old Persian language.
[3] The king's royal baton that indicated his authority as the ruler.

Chapter 1

In Times of Need

Indeed, you **CAN** come before the Ruler of the Universe at any time. The full citation from Hebrews 4:16 reads as follows:

> *Let us then approach God's throne of grace with confidence, so that we may receive mercy and find grace to help us in our time of need.*

You can come to God, particularly when you have a special need; He is always ready to help. The key word here is "need," a need that only God can take care of. God is not to be treated like a genie or Santa Claus. We do not come to God with a wish list, because a wish list reflects our selfish desires, things we want to have. A need is something for which we do not have good human solutions. In some situations, there may be no human solution available. Let us look at two examples of how people's needs are met through the Real Faith:

> *In those days Hezekiah became ill and was at the point of death. The prophet[4] Isaiah son of Amoz went to him and said, "This is what the LORD says: Put your house in order, because you are going to die; you will not recover." Hezekiah turned his face to the wall and prayed to the LORD, "Remember, LORD, how I have walked before you faithfully and with wholehearted devotion and have done what is good in your eyes." And Hezekiah wept bitterly. Before Isaiah had left the middle court, the word of the LORD came to him: "Go back and tell Hezekiah, the ruler of my people, 'This is what the LORD, the God of your father David, says: I have heard your prayer and seen your tears; I will heal you'"* (2 Kings 20:1–5), *and "I will add fifteen years to your life"* (Isaiah 38:5).

Hezekiah was too sick to even sit up for prayer. But he prayed from his heart, facing the wall while lying in his bed. He was the

---

[4] Someone who brings a message from God and also tells the future under God's guidance.

king of the land of Judah, but he came before God with great humility. While praying to God, Hezekiah cried just like a baby would. God did not turn him away. God healed him of his terrible disease, and he lived for 15 more years. Without the Real Faith, Hezekiah was soon going to die.

In the book of Acts, we have this account:

> *It was about this time that King Herod arrested some who belonged to the church[5], intending to persecute[6] them. He had James, the brother of John, put to death with the sword. So Peter was kept in prison, but the church was earnestly praying to God for him. The night before Herod was to bring him to trial, Peter was sleeping between two soldiers, bound with two chains, and sentries stood guard at the entrance. Suddenly an angel[7] of the Lord appeared and a light shone in the cell. He struck Peter on the side and woke him up. "Quick, get up!" he said, and the chains fell off Peter's wrists. Then the angel said to him, "Put on your clothes and sandals." And Peter did so. "Wrap your cloak around you and follow me," the angel told him. They passed the first and second guards and came to the iron gate leading to the city. It opened for them by itself, and they went through it. When they had walked the length of one street, suddenly the angel left him* (Acts 12:1-2, 5–8, 10).

Peter had been a follower of Jesus, and now he was preaching the message of Jesus to others. He was kept in the maximum security prison of that time with three levels of security and chains around his wrists. When King Herod was about to bring Peter out of the prison during the night, it was not to let him go free. No!

---

[5] An assembly of people who are followers of Jesus.
[6] To bully and mistreat the followers of Jesus.
[7] A heavenly being sent out from God's throne.

Peter was going to be killed. Herod had already killed James, another follower of Jesus. Now it was Peter's turn. He could not have escaped death without help from the throne of God.

The angel helped Peter out of the prison because the church—the people who had the Real Faith—earnestly prayed to God. They approached the throne of God with confidence in their time of need, because Peter, their leader, was put in prison by a cruel king.

The Greatest Need

The greatest need of all, which every person has, is to receive forgiveness from God for the sins we have committed. There are no exceptions, because *all have sinned ...* (Romans 3:23). Sin is acting against the commandments[8] of God, and every person has been guilty of disobeying God's commandments. Therefore, forgiveness must be obtained. But why is forgiveness the greatest need? It is because *people are destined to die once, and after that to face judgment ...* (Hebrews 9:27). *We must all appear before the judgment seat of Christ*[9] *...* (2 Corinthians 5:10) to receive punishment for our sins unless we have been forgiven.

Mercy and Grace

You can come to God's throne of grace to receive forgiveness. You can also come to Him when you have a need that only He can take care of.

Let us then approach God's throne of grace ... so that we may receive mercy and find grace ... (Hebrews 4:16). By coming to the throne of God in prayer and with humility, we obtain two things: mercy and grace. Whether some special need is taken care of or not is God's to decide, but we can be sure of receiving His mercy and grace.

---

[8] Rules of living that God has given to us.
[9] Jesus, who was the Messiah—the One who came to deliver humanity from their sins.

Mercy

Mercy refers to God's love and kindness. No matter what, God loves those who come to Him. Actually, God comes near to those who come to Him with total humility. James wrote, *Submit yourselves, then, to God. ... Come near to God and he will come near to you* (James 4:7-8).

God loves you even before you come to Him. And He looks at you with kindness. Here is a story that Jesus once told to give an example of mercy:

> *The kingdom of heaven is like a king who wanted to settle accounts with his servants. As he began the settlement, a man who owed him ten thousand bags of gold was brought to him. Since he was not able to pay, the master ordered that he and his wife and his children and all that he had be sold to repay the debt. At this the servant fell on his knees before him. "Be patient with me," he begged, "and I will pay back everything." The servant's master took pity on him, canceled the debt and let him go* (Matthew 18:23–27).

The master of the servant showed mercy and forgave what was owed to him. He canceled the punishment his servant had deserved. God, too, takes pity on us and cancels our huge debt of sin. He forgives us when we come to Him asking for His mercy. We also obtain His mercy when we present to Him other needs that only He can take care of.

Grace

Grace is what God does for humans out of His goodness and lovingkindness. No matter what, we can be sure that God's grace is sufficient for all of our needs. God says, *"My grace is sufficient for you ..."* (2 Corinthians 12:9).

God's grace helps us through our problems. It helps us to continue on, even in difficult situations. But, above all, our sins are forgiven by God's grace.

Chapter 1

God's grace flows out of His mercy. By His grace, God forgives us, no matter what we have done. There is no sin that God cannot forgive, if we come to Him with humility just as King Hezekiah did.

Here is an account from the life of Jesus who was *full of grace and truth* (John 1:14). Some religious leaders one day brought before Jesus a woman who was caught in sin. They said to Jesus, *"In the Law Moses commanded us to stone such women. Now what do you say?"* (8:5).

> Jesus did not give them an answer. Instead, He *bent down and started to write on the ground with his finger. When they kept on questioning him, he straightened up and said to them, "Let any one of you who is without sin be the first to throw a stone at her." Again he stooped down and wrote on the ground. At this, those who heard began to go away one at a time, the older ones first, until only Jesus was left, with the woman still standing there. Jesus straightened up and asked her, "Woman, where are they? Has no one condemned you?" "No one, sir," she said. "Then neither do I condemn you," Jesus declared. "Go now and leave your life of sin"* (8: 6–11).

No one knows for sure what Jesus wrote on the ground, but there is a clue. What Jesus wrote found each one who was ready to throw stones at the woman guilty of their own sins. If we guess that Jesus wrote the sins of everyone who was present, that would be a good guess.

Once everyone's sin had been pointed out, they all left, one by one, after Jesus said, *"Let any one of you who is without sin be the first to throw a stone at her"* (8:7). They were found guilty by Jesus, every single one, because no one is without sin. The only one left was the woman. Jesus asked her, *"Has no one condemned you?"* (8:10). The woman answered, *"No one, sir"* (8:11). The word "sir" in the original language also means "lord." The woman called Jesus her Lord, and she received forgiveness. Jesus sent her away forgiven when He said, *"Then neither do I condemn you ... Go now and leave your life of sin"* (8:11).

The Way

The songwriter[10] says, *"Taste and see that the LORD is good"* (Psalms 34:8). When you come across an unknown food, you first want to taste it to see if you would like it. The LORD God throws out a challenge to everyone. He assures you that if you will just come to Him, you will find Him to be good, kind, and loving. That's why He wants you to come before Him with your needs, and receive His mercy and grace. But, to come to Him, proper decorum is necessary.

To approach God, you do not need any special clothes. You do not need to put together any special words. No particular language is required. You do not need to memorize some mysterious chant or mantra[11]. No special ceremonies are necessary. You do not have to take a journey to a specific place. You do not have to perform any particular works. No special permissions are needed. Actually, all such efforts are totally useless.

Once again, we read in Hebrews 4:16, *Let us then approach God's throne of grace with confidence ... .* You can come to the throne of God boldly, with great confidence and full assurance.

Where do you get this confidence to come to the King of the Universe? The answer is: through Jesus Christ.

When you come with humility to Jesus Christ, He opens the way to God's throne in Heaven. There is no other way. You may or may not like it. You may or may not want to believe it. But, this is the truth because Jesus Himself said it.

Jesus said, *"I am the way and the truth and the life. No one comes to the Father except through me"* (John 14:6). This is not just a statement that Jesus made. It is also a warning—a warning to

---

[10] Psalmist.
[11] Repetitious verbal formulas, generally in a language that is not commonly used.

everyone in the world—that there is no other way. Because there is only one way, this also means that there is only one Real Faith.

When Jesus said, *"No one comes to the Father except through me"* (14:6), the Father to whom Jesus referred was God, sitting on His throne. Anyone can come before the throne, in any condition, at any place, at any time. But, you must come before God through humble prayer in the name of Jesus. Why Jesus is the only way is explained further in the next two chapters.

Conclusion

The Real Faith helps you come to God without fear to receive His mercy and grace. It does not matter who you are; you can come to God. The way has been opened for you by Jesus Christ. You can come before God's throne to receive His forgiveness and to present any special needs you may have. Come to Him; He is waiting for you.

CHAPTER 2

Given to Us

This chapter will explain why Jesus is the only way to God's throne. You will learn who Jesus is, why He came into this world, and how we must relate to Him.

Who Is Jesus?

Many people around the world have heard the name of Jesus, but many have not. Actually, a lot of people do not really know who Jesus is. Some believe He was a prophet, whereas others think He was a good teacher. But, Jesus is far more than a mere prophet or a good teacher.

Before Jesus was born in this world, He was called the Word:

> *In the beginning was the Word, and the Word was with God, and the Word was God. He was with God in the beginning. Through him all things were made; without him nothing was made that has been made. The Word became flesh and made his dwelling among us* (John 1:1–3, 14).

The Word—who is Jesus—existed from the very beginning. He existed even before His birth in Bethlehem. He Himself said, *"Before Abraham was born, I am!"* (8:58). Abraham lived roughly

2,000 years before Jesus was born. Yet, Jesus said that He existed before Abraham. Was He telling the truth?

The Word became flesh and made his dwelling among us (1:14). John, the beloved disciple[12] of Jesus, wrote that the Word became flesh, or human, and lived among the common people. Jesus is the Word, who became human. Just think about this.

The Word was there with God in the beginning. Then the Word became human. This can mean only one thing: The Word, Jesus, was not human before His birth.

There is a reason why Jesus was called the Word before He came to this Earth. John wrote: *Through him all things were made; without him nothing was made that has been made* (1:3). The Word was the Creator, who made all things. This is how He created everything: *He spoke, and it came to be; he commanded, and it stood firm* (Psalms 33:9). Jesus, the Word, created all things by simply speaking His word, and in an instant, it was done. Hence, when Jesus said, *"Before Abraham was born, I am!"* (John 8:38), He was telling the truth.

The LORD Is One

The Word was with God, and the Word was God (John 1:1). How can the Word (Jesus) be with God and Himself be God? There is only one possibility: God is not a single person. In simple terms, we can think of God as a family. In the Holy Scriptures, the term "Deity" or "Godhead" is used to refer to the God family.

Now, one person is someone who is single or alone. Two people together form a couple. A family has more than two people. So, the Godhead—the God family—has more than two Persons.[13] Yet, the Deity or Godhead is one God—one God family.

When answering a question, Jesus once pointed to what is written in Deuteronomy 6:4: *The Lord our God, the Lord is one* (Mark 12:29).

---

[12] Close follower of Jesus.
[13] The one Godhead includes three distinct Persons—the Word, the Father, and the Holy Spirit. This is discussed more fully in Chapter 7.

Chapter 2

There is one big difference between human families and the Godhead. In human families, there are often disagreements about various things. Within the same family, sometimes people do not get along with each other. Among the three Persons of the Godhead, however, there is always complete agreement. That is the nature of God. Knowledge about the nature of God is essential for a correct understanding of the Holy Scriptures.

When Deuteronomy 6:4 says, *The LORD is one*, it is not referring to God as just being one in number. God is one in two other ways:

First, the one God means that there is no other God besides the One whom Jesus has made known. Since ancient times, people have worshiped different gods who have been given their own names. But, Jesus has made known to us the One and only God. On one occasion, Jesus was telling people who did not want to believe in Him, *"How can you believe since you ... do not seek the glory that comes from the only God?"* (John 5:44). Jesus' reference to the only God means that there is no other God besides the One revealed by Jesus.

Second, the idea of one God refers to unity. The God family is one in perfect unity. The unity among the three persons of the Godhead cannot be any more perfect than what it is. The apostles[14] Paul and Timothy referred to the perfection, the closeness, and the oneness of the Godhead when they used the term, *the fullness of the Deity,* in Colossians 2:9. And not only that, but also, *in Christ all the fullness of the Deity lives in bodily form* (2:9). So, Jesus is the fullness of the Godhead. He is fully God. On that basis, Jesus boldly declared, *"I and the Father are one"* (John 10:30). Jesus also came to this Earth as a complete human being, and He referred to God as His father.

It should not be surprising that the One and only Deity has been revealed in the person of Jesus Christ. John wrote: *No one*

---

[14] Apostle: Someone who was sent out to take Jesus' teachings to others.

has ever seen God, but the one and only Son, who is himself God and is in closest relationship with the Father, has made him known (1:18).

Many people did not believe Jesus when He said that He and the Father were one. So, again He said, *"Believe me when I say that I am in the Father and the Father is in me ..."* (14:11). This is how close Jesus and the Father are. It is as if they were one person. This is also the reason why Jesus is the only way to the throne of God.

Given to Us

God is sinless and holy. Sin and holiness do not mix; they are opposites. Because of our sin, it was impossible for us to come to God. But, it was because of His great love for sinful humans that God came to us. *The Word became flesh and made his dwelling among us* (John 1:14).

About 700 years before Jesus came into this world, the prophet Isaiah gave this prophecy[15]:

> *For to us a child is born, to us a son is given, and the government will be on his shoulders. And he will be called Wonderful Counselor, Mighty God, Everlasting Father, Prince of Peace. Of the greatness of his government and peace there will be no end* (Isaiah 9:6, 7).

The child in this prophecy is Jesus. Indeed, Jesus was given to us as a gift from God. Without Him, everyone would have perished[16] without any hope of salvation[17]. In the ancient book of Isaiah, Jesus is called the Mighty God and Everlasting Father.

The prophet Isaiah also wrote: *The virgin will conceive and give birth to a son, and will call him Immanuel* (7:14). The Hebrew name "Immanuel" means *God with us* (Matthew 1:23). Jesus was born of

---

[15] A message from God that may also include future events told before they happen, under Heavenly guidance.

[16] To perish: To die under the condemnation of sin, and without any hope of salvation.

[17] Freedom from the condemnation of sin, and the assurance of God's gift of eternal life.

Chapter 2

a virgin, Mary. The Word, who was God, came to Earth to be with us.

Born to Be the Son

When the angel Gabriel visited Mary, He announced to her:

> "Do not be afraid, Mary; you have found favor with God. You will conceive and give birth to a son, and you are to call him Jesus. So the holy one to be born will be called the Son of God" (Luke 1:30-31, 35).

Jesus, as a human, was born of God. He had no human father. That is why He is called the Son of God. Only once in the history of this world, God was born as a baby in the person of Jesus Christ. This had never happened before Jesus came, and it will never happen again. Jesus Christ was unique, the only One born of God the Father.

What the Disciples Knew

Jesus once asked His disciples about who other people thought He was. *They replied, "Some say John the Baptist; others say Elijah; and still others, Jeremiah or one of the prophets"* (Matthew 16:14). People had opinions that Jesus was like one of the other prophets.

Jesus then asked His disciples, *"But what about you?" ... "Who do you say I am?"* (16:15). Jesus was eager to know if His own close followers had understood who He was, unlike other people who thought that He was just like another prophet.

Without any doubt in his mind, *Simon Peter answered, "You are the Messiah,*[18] *the Son of the living God"* (16:16). *Jesus replied, "Blessed are you, Simon son of Jonah, for this was not revealed to you by flesh and blood,*[19] *but by my Father in heaven"* (16:17).

After spending a little more than three years with Jesus, many of His followers had understood that He was the Son of God—God

---

[18] Christ. It was commonly known among the Jewish people that the Messiah would be the Son of God, and would be from the line of King David.
[19] Humans.

who came as a human. Jesus said to Peter, *"This was ... revealed to you ... by my Father in heaven* (16:17). Even today, it is only by God's Spirit that we can understand that Jesus truly is the Son of the living God. This is because the natural sinful mind cannot understand the things of God.

Two Eyewitnesses

John wrote: *We have seen his glory, the glory of the one and only Son, who came from the Father, full of grace and truth* (John 1:14).

One day, Jesus took three of his close followers—Peter, James, and John—to the top of a high mountain. *There he was transfigured before them. His face shone like the sun, and his clothes became as white as the light* (Matthew 17:2). This is the glory that His followers saw. Then a bright cloud covered Peter, James, and John, *and a voice from the cloud said, "This is my Son, whom I love; with him I am well pleased. Listen to him!" When the disciples heard this, they fell facedown to the ground, terrified. But Jesus came and touched them. "Get up," he said. "Don't be afraid"* (17:5–7). Like the disciples, we can also be in the presence of God the Father and not be afraid when Jesus is on our side.

The apostle Peter was an eyewitness[20] to the majesty of Jesus. Later, Peter wrote two letters to the believers[21] in Jesus. In one of the letters, he wrote:

> *We did not follow cleverly devised stories when we told you about the coming of our Lord Jesus Christ in power, but we were eyewitnesses of his majesty. He received honor and glory from God the Father when the voice came to him from the Majestic Glory, saying, "This is my Son, whom I love; with him I am well pleased." We ourselves heard this voice that came from heaven when we were with him on the sacred mountain"* (2 Peter 1:16–18).

---

[20] Someone who has seen certain things and events with his/her own eyes.
[21] Those who have made a commitment to follow Jesus.

Peter related to the believers his personal experience on the mountain. He taught that Jesus was the Christ, the Son of the living God—that He was God who came as a human. To set the record straight, Peter made it clear that he was present on the holy mountain, he saw Jesus' glory, and he heard the voice of God the Father confirming the majesty of Jesus. It was not some made-up story. It was the truth, to which Peter was an eyewitness.

John was also an eyewitness on the same mountain along with Peter. He wrote: *We have seen his glory, the glory of the one and only Son, who came from the Father ...* (John 1:14). So, there are two eyewitnesses who tell us exactly the same thing. They both saw the glory of Jesus as the Son of God.

Two eyewitnesses telling the same thing would be sufficient today in a court of law. Hence, we should be able to believe the two eyewitnesses, Peter and John.

The Only Name

Jesus was born into a Jewish home. He was given the Hebrew name, Yeshua, which means "salvation." In English, the translated name for Yeshua is Jesus. When the angel announced to Joseph that Mary would have a son, the angel said, *"She will give birth to a son, and you are to give him the name Jesus, because he will save his people from their sins"* (Matthew 1:21).

Jesus is the only One who can free us from the condemnation[22] of sin. *Salvation is found in no one else, for there is no other name under heaven given to mankind by which we must be saved* (Acts 4:12).

He Came for All

In God's eyes, there is only one race on this Earth—the human race. Jesus came for the entire human race. Jesus opened the way for you to come to God, regardless of who you are or where you live in the world.

---

[22] Punishment after a person is found guilty in a judgment.

In Chapter 1, you learned that the greatest need—which every human has—is forgiveness of sin because *all have sinned* (Romans 3:23). Jesus came for one purpose, as we read:

> *Here is a trustworthy saying that deserves full acceptance: Christ Jesus came into the world to save sinners ...*
> (1 Timothy 1:15).

We are all sinners, and Jesus came for all of us. He came for every person in the world. He came for those who accept Him, and even for those who do not accept Him. His mercy and grace are available to all, but there is one condition. You must come to Him.

He Came to Save

John wrote: *God did not send his Son into the world to condemn the world, but to save the world through him* (John 3:17). The world can be saved only through Jesus.

We find nowhere else that someone ever came into this world to save sinners, not even one sinner. Jesus is the only One, and He came for all sinners. No one else ever had the power to forgive sins; only Jesus has that power. Jesus said, *"All authority in heaven and on earth has been given to me"* (Matthew 28:18).

In Chapter 1, you read about the sinful woman whom Jesus forgave; it is recorded in John 8:3–11. Here is another account of forgiveness, as recorded in Matthew 9:2–7:

> *Some men brought to him a paralyzed man, lying on a mat. When Jesus saw their faith, he said to the man, "Take heart, son; your sins are forgiven."*
>
> *At this, some of the teachers of the law said to themselves, "This fellow is blaspheming!"*[23]
>
> *Knowing their thoughts, Jesus said, "Why do you entertain evil thoughts in your hearts? Which is easier: to say,*

---

[23] Taking God's place (in forgiving sins).

Chapter 2

> *'Your sins are forgiven,' or to say, 'Get up and walk'? But I want you to know that the Son of Man has authority on earth to forgive sins."* So he said to the paralyzed man, *"Get up, take your mat and go home."* Then the man got up and went home.

It would be easy for someone to say, "Your sins are forgiven." But, it is not at all easy to tell a very sick person to get up and walk. Jesus showed that He had the power to forgive sins when he told the man who was paralyzed and could not even move his body, *"Get up, take your mat and go home"* (9:6). From that time, this man's life was changed. Jesus performed many wonderful works to show that He was God who had come to Earth to forgive sins and to change people's lives for the better. He does the same today.

Very seldom did Jesus make Himself known as the Son of God. Most of the time, He identified Himself with humanity by calling Himself the Son of Man. It was up to the people to recognize that He was truly the Son of God—God who came as a man. Many people had some idea that Jesus was the Messiah—the Son of God—but they did not believe in Him. People had the choice either to believe in Him or not believe in Him. You have the same choice now.

Jesus came that through Him you may receive forgiveness for your sins. Without His forgiveness, you cannot be saved from condemnation. You cannot undo sin by doing good works or living a good life. To receive salvation, you cannot go to some religious "holy" place, and you cannot get it from some other person. Jesus is the only way.

To Whoever Believes

One of the most well-known Scriptures is John 3:16: *God so loved the world that he gave his one and only Son, that whoever believes in him shall not perish but have eternal life*[24].

---

[24] Life without death. Living forever with God.

Forgiveness of sins brings eternal life—life without facing death. Living forever is what Jesus gives to anyone who believes in Him. *Whoever believes in him* in John 3:16 means that it does not matter who you are. You may be young or old. You may be rich or poor. You may or may not have formal education. You may think you are the worst of sinners. You may think you are beyond any hope of salvation. You may even think that you are a good person. You may think that you follow a certain religion. You may have no religion. You may think you were born in a religious family. You may go through certain religious rites, and you may take part in religious activities. All these things do not matter. Yes, not a single one of these things matters. As an individual, you need salvation through Jesus Christ. *If we claim to be without sin, we deceive ourselves and the truth is not in us* (1 John 1:8). So, do not be deceived.

Looking for the One

Because Jesus came to save sinners, He used to mingle with sinners. For this, He was criticized by the religious leaders who did not think they needed salvation.

> *Now the tax collectors and sinners were all gathering around to hear Jesus. But the Pharisees*[25] *and the teachers of the law muttered, "This man welcomes sinners and eats with them."*
>
> *Then Jesus told them this parable*[26]*: "Suppose one of you has a hundred sheep and loses one of them. Doesn't he leave the ninety-nine in the open country and go after the lost sheep until he finds it? And when he finds it, he joyfully puts it on his shoulders and goes home. Then he calls his friends and neighbors together and says, 'Rejoice with me; I have found my lost sheep.' I tell you that in the same way there will be more rejoicing in heaven over one*

---

[25] Pharisees belonged to a religious sect in the time of Jesus. Members of this sect thought that they had salvation because they were religious.

[26] A story that teaches a spiritual lesson.

sinner who repents[27] *than over ninety-nine righteous persons*[28] *who do not need to repent"* (Luke 15:1–7).

Jesus said, *"I am the good shepherd"* (John 10:11). He is searching for the lost sheep. Even if you were the only one lost out there, He is looking for you. Then Jesus stated, *"My sheep listen to my voice; I know them, and they follow me. I give them eternal life, and they shall never perish ...* (10:27-28). You can listen to His gentle voice today and follow Him. He is ready to give you eternal life if you will only come to Him and follow Him.

With Open Arms

Jesus told this story to help us understand what God is like:

> *"There was a man who had two sons. The younger one said to his father, 'Father, give me my share of the estate.' So he divided his property between them.*
>
> *"Not long after that, the younger son got together all he had, set off for a distant country and there squandered his wealth in wild living. After he had spent everything, there was a severe famine in that whole country, and he began to be in need. So he went and hired himself out to a citizen of that country, who sent him to his fields to feed pigs. He longed to fill his stomach with the pods that the pigs were eating, but no one gave him anything.*
>
> *"When he came to his senses, he said, 'How many of my father's hired servants have food to spare, and here I am starving to death! I will set out and go back to my father and say to him: Father, I have sinned against heaven and against you. I am no longer worthy to be called your son; make me like one of your hired servants.' So he got up and went to his father.*

---

[27] To confess your sins to God, and turn away from past sinful ways.

[28] Those who have repented of their sins and accepted Jesus, and live in obedience to His commands.

> "But while he was still a long way off, his father saw him and was filled with compassion for him; he ran to his son, threw his arms around him and kissed him.
>
> "The son said to him, 'Father, I have sinned against heaven and against you. I am no longer worthy to be called your son.'
>
> "But the father said to his servants, 'Quick! Bring the best robe and put it on him. Put a ring on his finger and sandals on his feet. ... Let's have a feast and celebrate. For this son of mine was dead and is alive again; he was lost and is found'" (Luke 15:11–24).

God is more loving than any human parent can be. He is not full of anger waiting to condemn us because we have sinned against Him. No! He is waiting with open arms to receive sinners if they will only turn from their sinful ways and come to Him. He is waiting for you to come home.

Conclusion

Jesus came to us because, on our own, we could not approach a Holy God. Now, He is looking for you and waiting for you to come to Him so He can forgive your sins. Believing in Jesus is the beginning of the Real Faith. You may be a good person in many ways. Still, without Jesus, you cannot have the Real Faith, and without the Real Faith, you cannot have eternal life.

You may ask, "What do I have to believe?" You must believe that Jesus is God who can forgive your sins and give you eternal life. *Whoever believes in the Son has eternal life, but whoever rejects the Son will not see life, for God's wrath remains on them* (John 3:36). The next chapter explains why you cannot come to God without Jesus.

CHAPTER 3

Why He Came

Jesus came for one purpose: to save sinners. He came to free us from the condemnation of sin. God could have left the world to perish, but He did not. Actually, He could not do that. Why?

God of Love

> *God is love. This is how God showed his love among us: He sent his one and only Son into the world that we might live through him. This is love: not that we loved God, but that he loved us and sent his Son as an atoning sacrifice[29] for our sins* (1 John 4:8–10).

We did not love God, but He loved us. He loves each one of us regardless of who we are. Why does God love us even though we are sinners? There is only one explanation: *God is love* (4:8). The God of love could not leave the world to perish. What an awesome God this is! Only in the Real Faith do we find that God is love and that He loves sinners. This is found nowhere else.

---

[29] Jesus' sacrifice that brings forgiveness of sins and makes it possible for us to come to God.

We actually became God's enemies because of sin. Through our disobedience, we went against God, we rebelled against Him, and we became His enemies. *While we were God's enemies, we were reconciled[30] to him through the death of his Son ...* (Romans 5:10). We were brought into the right relationship with God through the death of Jesus Christ. Jesus came because of God's love. That's the only reason why He came. The apostle Paul wanted the believers in Ephesus to understand God's love when he wrote, *how wide and long and high and deep is the love of Christ ... this love that surpasses knowledge* (Ephesians 3:18-19).

We became His enemies, but *God demonstrates his own love for us in this: While we were still sinners, Christ died for us* (5:8). Jesus gave His life so that *we might live through him* (1 John 4:9). This is how immense God's love is.

Without God's love, the entire human race would have perished. But, Jesus Christ came to save because of God's love for all people. *For God so loved the world that he gave his one and only Son ...* (John 3:16).

Put your own name in the blank spaces here: God so loved _____ that He gave Jesus to save _____. For sure, Jesus came just for you.

Now, sit back in a quiet place and think about it. What does this sentence mean to you with your own name in it?

Peace with Us

Let us just suppose for a moment that God was human, and that he was the ruler of a country. A neighboring country ruled by another king became a bitter enemy of God's country. If God was more powerful than the other king, what do you suppose he would do? Most likely, God would make war and destroy this other country. It is natural for humans to treat their enemies in this manner.

---

[30] Accepted by God and united with Him.

Chapter 3

But, God is not human. He is love. Because He loved us, He could not destroy us, even though we were His enemies. So, the only option He had was to make peace with us.

But, to make peace, He could not come down to us in His *Majestic Glory* (2 Peter 1:17). In His Heavenly glory, *God is a consuming fire* (Hebrews 12:29). It is impossible for any human to come face to face with God and live. That's why God came to us in the form of a human—in the person of Jesus Christ, as described in the previous chapter. In Jesus, the *Prince of Peace* (Isaiah 9:6), God came to Earth to make peace with us, His enemies.

Why the Cross

Why did Jesus give His life on the cross? To help us find peace with God.

> *For God was pleased to have all his fullness dwell in him, and through him to reconcile to himself all things ... by making peace through his blood, shed on the cross* (Colossians 1:19-20).

God is the one who took the first step to make peace with us. The only way to make peace with us was by sending Jesus to the cross. But, why?

Sin offends God. It is so serious that it causes separation from God, and there must be punishment for sin. Normally, the sinner is the one who should bear the punishment. The sinner could not just start obeying God to undo past sin. The only option for the sinner was to face death, to be finished, to be no more. There is nothing the sinner can do to have his/her sins forgiven. But, because of His love for the human race, God Himself paid the penalty for our sins by sending Jesus to the cross. In the sufferings of Jesus, God suffered on behalf of us all.

Before the Cross

Even before He went to the cross, Jesus suffered and endured humiliation.

The Prediction

Jesus said to his followers, *"As you know, the Passover is two days away—and the Son of Man will be handed over to be crucified"* (Matthew 26:2). He could see what was coming, and said, *"Now my soul is troubled, and what shall I say? 'Father, save me from this hour'? No, it was for this very reason I came to this hour* (John 12:27). Here, Jesus Himself said that it was for just one reason that He came: to give His life for the sins of the world.

Then the chief priests and the elders of the people assembled in the palace of the high priest, whose name was Caiaphas, and they schemed to arrest Jesus secretly and kill him (Matthew 26:3-4).

Anguish in Prayer

Jesus celebrated the Passover and ate the holy meal with His 12 disciples. After the meal, when it was night, *Jesus went with his disciples to a place called Gethsemane, and he said to them, "Sit here while I go over there and pray"* (Matthew 26:36). Gethsemane still exists today. It is a grove of olive trees located on the lower slope of the Mount of Olives, facing Jerusalem on the West. *Jesus had often met there with his disciples* (John 18:2).

> Jesus *began to be sorrowful and troubled. Then he said to them, "My soul is overwhelmed with sorrow to the point of death"* (Matthew 26:37-38). *Going a little farther, he fell with his face to the ground and prayed, "My Father, if it is possible, may this cup be taken from me.*[31] *Yet not as I will, but as you will"* (26:39). *And being in anguish, he prayed more earnestly, and his sweat was like drops of blood falling to the ground* (Luke 22:44). *He went away*

---

[31] His suffering and death by crucifixion.

Chapter 3

> *a second time and prayed, "My Father, if it is not possible for this cup to be taken away unless I drink it, may your will be done"* (Matthew 26:42). Jesus then *prayed the third time, saying the same thing* (26:44).

As a human, Jesus wished that His sufferings would be taken away from Him. But, He prayed for God's will to be done. It was God's will that Jesus should go to the cross to save humanity, because there was no other way.

The Arrest

Soon after Jesus finished praying, there came *a large crowd armed with swords and clubs, sent from the chief priests and the elders of the people* (Matthew 26:47). *They were carrying torches, lanterns and weapons* (John 18:3). *Then the men stepped forward, seized Jesus and arrested him* (Matthew 26:50).

> *In that hour Jesus said to the crowd, "Am I leading a rebellion, that you have come out with swords and clubs to capture me? Every day I sat in the temple courts teaching, and you did not arrest me. But this has all taken place that the writings of the prophets might be fulfilled." Then all the disciples deserted him and fled* (26:55-56).

This happened in fulfillment of an ancient prophecy: *"Strike the shepherd, and the sheep will be scattered[32] ..."* (Zechariah 13:7). Jesus quoted this prophecy when he told his disciples at the Passover meal, *"This very night you will all fall away on account of me ..."* (Matthew 26:31).

Unfair Trial

At the trial of Jesus, the chief priests did not follow the teachings of their own law: *Follow justice and justice alone ...* (Deuteronomy 16:20).

---

[32] The prophet Zechariah wrote this prophecy more than 500 years before the crucifixion of Jesus.

Those who had arrested Jesus took him to Caiaphas the high priest, where the teachers of the law and the elders had assembled.

The chief priests and the whole Sanhedrin[33] were looking for false evidence against Jesus so that they could put him to death. But they did not find any ... (Matthew 26:57, 59-60).

Many testified falsely against him, but their statements did not agree (Mark 14:56).

Then the high priest stood up and said to Jesus, "Are you not going to answer? What is this testimony that these men are bringing against you?" But Jesus remained silent (Matthew 26:62-63).

Then, the high priest said to him, "I charge you under oath by the living God: Tell us if you are the Messiah, the Son of God."

"You have said so," Jesus replied. "But I say to all of you: From now on you will see the Son of Man sitting at the right hand of the Mighty One and coming on the clouds of heaven" (26:63-64).

Then the high priest tore his clothes[34] and said, "He has spoken blasphemy[35]! Why do we need any more witnesses? Look, now you have heard the blasphemy. What do you think?" "He is worthy of death," they answered (26:65-66).

Jesus' teachings were against the pretentions and man-made traditions of the Jewish leaders. So the chief priests, the teachers of the Jewish law, and the elders had become Jesus' enemies. Justice was corrupted when false witnesses were called against Jesus. According to the writings of the prophets, the Messiah would be

---

[33] The ancient Jewish supreme council or religious court in Jerusalem.
[34] A religious act when something offensive was heard or seen.
[35] Speaking evil of God, or taking the place of God.

Chapter 3

the Son of God.[36] So, the high priest asked Jesus if He was the Messiah, the Son of God. Jesus had spoken the truth when He said, *"You have said so"* (Matthew 26:64). But, those who were spiritually blind saw it as blasphemy.

> *Then they spit in his face and struck him with their fists. Others slapped him ... (26:67).*
>
> *And they said many other insulting things to him (Luke 22:65).*
>
> *And the guards took him and beat him (Mark 14:65).*
>
> *Early in the morning, all the chief priests and the elders of the people made their plans how to have Jesus executed[37]. So they bound him, led him away and handed him over to Pilate the governor (Matthew 27:1-2).*
>
> *When he was accused by the chief priests and the elders, he gave no answer. Then Pilate asked him, "Don't you hear the testimony they are bringing against you?" But Jesus made no reply, not even to a single charge—to the great amazement of the governor (27:12–14).*

Approximately 700 years before these events, the prophet Isaiah wrote: *He was oppressed and afflicted, yet he did not open his mouth; he was led like a lamb to the slaughter, and as a sheep before its shearers is silent, so he did not open his mouth* (Isaiah 53:7). This prophecy was fulfilled, exactly as written.

An Upset Governor

At one point, Pilate got upset with the chief priests. He said, *"Take him yourselves and judge him by your own law"* (John 18:31). According to the Jewish law, the punishment for blasphemy was death by stoning, not crucifixion. But, the Jews could not stone someone to death during the holy season of Passover. So, they complained to Pilate, *"But we have no right to execute anyone"* (18:31).

---

[36] Psalm 2 presents this understanding quite straightforwardly.
[37] Put to death.

This took place to fulfill what Jesus had said about the kind of death he was going to die (18:32). For example, Jesus had said that *the Son of Man must be lifted up, that everyone who believes may have eternal life in him* (3:14-15). Only under the Roman law could Jesus be lifted up on a cross.

Jesus' death by crucifixion also fulfilled a prophecy written approximately 1,000 years before it happened. David, who was a king and a prophet, wrote in Psalm 22:16: *A pack of villains encircles me; they pierce my hands and my feet*. David did not write this about himself, because he died a natural death. Isaiah also wrote: *He was pierced for our transgressions*[38] (Isaiah 53:5). These prophecies about the crucifixion of the Messiah had to be fulfilled, and they were fulfilled, exactly as written.

Failed Plan to Free Jesus

Now it was the governor's custom at the festival[39] *to release a prisoner chosen by the crowd* (Matthew 27:15). *A man called Barabbas was in prison with the insurrectionists who had committed murder in the uprising* (Mark 15:7). *So when the crowd had gathered, Pilate asked them, "Which one do you want me to release to you: Jesus Barabbas,*[40] *or Jesus who is called the Messiah?"* (Matthew 27:17). *But the chief priests stirred up the crowd to have Pilate release Barabbas instead* (Mark 15:11). *Wanting to satisfy the crowd, Pilate released Barabbas to them* (15:15).

Humiliation

Then Pilate took Jesus and had him flogged[41]. *The soldiers twisted together a crown of thorns and put it on his head. They clothed him in a purple robe ...* (John 19:1-2). *Again and again they struck him on*

---

[38] Sins.
[39] The feast of Passover.
[40] Jesus was a common enough name. So, the full name of Barabbas would be translated as "Jesus, son of daddy."
[41] Beaten with the Roman whip made of leather straps with pieces of metal or bone at the end.

the head with a staff and spit on him (Mark 15:19). *And they slapped him in the face* (John 19:3). Jesus endured all this without saying a word.

Crucify! Crucify!

> *Wanting to release Jesus, Pilate appealed to them* (Luke 23:20) one last time. *Pilate came out and said to the Jews gathered there, "Look, I am bringing him out to you to let you know that I find no basis for a charge against him." When Jesus came out wearing the crown of thorns and the purple robe, Pilate said to them, "Here is the man!" But, as soon as the chief priests and their officials saw him, they shouted, "Crucify! Crucify!"* (John 19:4–6).

Pilate had thought that after the people would see how badly Jesus had been flogged, with blood running all over His body, they would be satisfied with His punishment. So Pilate brought Jesus out and said, *"Here is the man!"* (19:5), or "See for yourselves that the man has been punished enough." *But they kept shouting, "Crucify him! Crucify him!"* (Luke 23:21).

Finally Pilate handed him over to them to be crucified (John 19:16). *After they had mocked him, they took off the robe and put his own clothes on him. Then they led him away to crucify him* (Matthew 27:31).

On the Cross

So the soldiers took charge of Jesus. Carrying his own cross, he went out to the place of the Skull (which in Aramaic[42] is called Golgotha[43]). There they crucified him ... (John 19:16–18). *A large number of people followed him, including women who mourned and wailed for him. Jesus turned and said to them, "... do not weep for me; weep for yourselves and for your children"* (Luke 23:27-28).

---

[42] The common language spoken in Jesus' day.
[43] Also called Calvary, from Latin.

Essentially, Jesus was saying, "There is no need to weep for Me because I am doing what I came to do, to save those who will believe in Me. Rather, weep for yourselves and your children. They may not believe in Me and receive the salvation I came to give."

It was nine in the morning when they crucified him (Mark 15:25). Large nails were driven through his hands and feet as He lay tied on the cross. *Jesus said, "Father, forgive them, for they do not know what they are doing"* (Luke 23:34). After driving the nails, the soldiers raised the cross upright and put it into a hole dug up in the ground.

> *They crucified two rebels with him, one on his right and one on his left* (Mark 15:27).
>
> *One of the criminals who hung there hurled insults at him: "Aren't you the Messiah? Save yourself and us!"*
>
> *But the other criminal rebuked him. "Don't you fear God," he said, "since you are under the same sentence? We are punished justly, for we are getting what our deeds deserve. But this man has done nothing wrong."*
>
> *Then he said, "Jesus, remember me when you come into your kingdom."*
>
> *Jesus answered him, "... you will be with me in paradise"* (Luke 23:39–43).

There will always be two types of people: one will accept Jesus' mercy and grace, and His offer of salvation; the other will reject Him, and even mock Him.

Another wonderful thing that Jesus did from the cross was to remember His mother. He asked His beloved disciple, John, to take care of His mother. This implies that Mary's husband, Joseph, whom she married after the birth of Jesus, had already died. John himself recorded:

> *Near the cross of Jesus stood his mother, his mother's sister, Mary the wife of Clopas, and Mary Magdalene.*

Chapter 3

> *When Jesus saw his mother there, and the disciple whom he loved standing nearby, he said to her, "Woman, here is your son," and to the disciple, "Here is your mother." From that time on, this disciple took her into his home* (John 19:25–27).

It was now about noon, and darkness came over the whole land until three in the afternoon, for the sun stopped shining (Luke 23:44-45). *About three in the afternoon Jesus cried out in a loud voice, "Eli, Eli, lema sabachthani?" (which means "My God, my God, why have you forsaken me?")* [Matthew 27:46]. This was also an exact prophecy given in Psalm 22:1.

God made him who had no sin to be sin for us ... (2 Corinthians 5:21). Jesus felt the crushing burden of all of humanity's sins that were placed on Him. The Holy Father could not look upon sin, and turned His face away. Deep down Jesus felt abandoned by His Father. He could not even refer to Him as His Father, the way He had always done. Feeling the separation and loneliness caused by the weight of sin upon Him, Jesus cried out the most agonizing cry let out from His spirit: *"My God, my God, why have you forsaken me?"* (Psalms 22:1). Jesus' cry tells us that sin offends God, and it separates us from God. But, through Jesus, we can be accepted by God and be united with Him. This is because, on the cross, Jesus paid the full penalty for our sins.

> *Later, knowing that everything had now been finished, and so that Scripture would be fulfilled, Jesus said, "I am thirsty"* (John 19:28). *Immediately one of them ran and got a sponge. He filled it with wine vinegar, put it on a staff, and offered it to Jesus to drink* (Matthew 27:48).

This fulfilled another ancient prophecy: *They ... gave me vinegar for my thirst* (Psalms 69:21). *When he had received the drink, Jesus said, "It is finished"* (John 19:30). The main purpose for which Jesus had come was now done. By His blood, He had purchased the salvation of every man, woman, and child.

Soon after, *Jesus called out with a loud voice, "Father, into your hands I commit my spirit." When he had said this, he breathed his last*[44] (Luke 23:46). The prophet Isaiah had written: *He poured out his life unto death ...* (Isaiah 53:12). Now, certain that He had fulfilled God's will, He again referred to God as Father.

When Jesus died on the cross, *the earth shook* and *the rocks split* (Matthew 27:51). *When the centurion*[45] *and those with him who were guarding Jesus saw the earthquake and all that had happened, they were terrified, and exclaimed, "Surely he was the Son of God!"* (Matthew 27:54). The Roman soldiers who had crucified Jesus became afraid that they had killed the Son of God.

John was an eyewitness of the crucifixion. After giving an account of what he saw and heard, he wrote: *The man who saw it has given testimony, and his testimony is true. He knows that he tells the truth, and he testifies so that you also may believe* (John 19:35).

Meaning of the Cross

Why did Jesus let Himself be crucified? Although He was God, Jesus lived as a human. He referred to God the Father as His Father. He set aside His Godly nature to fulfill the purpose for which He came to Earth: to give His life for our salvation. There is nothing that we could have done to save ourselves from our sins.

Jesus bled and suffered the most severe pain imaginable on the cross for six hours, from about nine in the morning until about three in the afternoon. He gave His life on the cross. But, was it necessary? *He committed no sin, and no deceit was found in his mouth"* (1 Peter 2:22). Jesus had never sinned. He was the only person who ever lived on this Earth without committing any sin. No one since has lived without sin. On one occasion, Jesus challenged the Jews who were arguing with Him: *"Can any of you prove me guilty of sin?"* (John 8:46). No one could point a finger at Him.

---

[44] He died.
[45] An officer in charge of 100 soldiers in the Roman army.

Chapter 3

At the time of His arrest in Gethsemane, *one of Jesus' companions reached for his sword, drew it out and struck the servant of the high priest ...* (Matthew 26:51). Jesus said, *"Put your sword back in its place ... . Do you think I cannot call on my Father, and he will at once put at my disposal more than twelve legions of angels?"* (26:52-53). One legion would be 6,000 angels.[46] No human army on Earth could stand against 72,000 (twelve legions) angels. If Jesus wanted to, He could have called the angels of Heaven on his side. Later, when Jesus was before Pilate, the governor said, *"Don't you realize I have power either to free you or to crucify you?"* Jesus answered, *"You would have no power over me if it were not given to you from above"* (John 19:10-11). Had Jesus used His divine[47] powers to free Himself, He would have failed to fulfill God's will. Humanity would have been lost forever in sin.

Jesus once said, *"I am the good shepherd ... and I lay down my life for the sheep. No one takes it from me, but I lay it down of my own accord"* (John 10:14, 15, 18). Jesus is our shepherd; He laid down His life for us. No one forced Jesus to give His life. He did it on His own, for you and for me. This was God's purpose, and Jesus came to fulfill it. That's why He prayed to God in Gethsemane, *"Not as I will, but as you will"* (Matthew 26:39).

God made him who had no sin to be sin for us ... (2 Corinthians 5:21). God laid all our sins upon Jesus. He died in our place, so we could be forgiven. The prophet Isaiah wrote: *The LORD has laid on him the iniquity of us all* (Isaiah 53:6), and further, *he was pierced for our transgressions, he was crushed for our iniquities; the punishment that brought us peace was on him ...* (53:5). The only way for God to forgive us and take our sins away was by letting Jesus, the Sinless One, carry our sins and bear the punishment for them. God Himself paid for the sins committed by all people. Thus, forgiveness is available to all those who by faith accept Jesus' sacrifice on their behalf. This is why it is only through Jesus that you can come to the throne of God to receive forgiveness.

---

[46] In the Roman army, 6,000 soldiers made up a legion.
[47] Of the same nature as God.

A sinful person cannot undo his own sins, let alone the sins of others. In the history of this world, many came and started their own religions. Many of these were good men. But, not one of them could pay the penalty for his own sins, let alone the sins of others. This is why Jesus is the only way for receiving forgiveness and having peace with God. Jesus is the only One who has the power to forgive sins.

> *God was reconciling the world to himself in Christ, not counting people's sins against them* (2 Corinthians 5:19).

Through His death on the cross, Jesus won us back to God. This is why we can come before the throne of God through Jesus. When our sins are forgiven, God no longer looks at our sins; He looks at Jesus. In a manner of speaking, through Jesus, God puts on us *a robe of his righteousness*[48] (Isaiah 61:10). God calls us righteous when our sins have been forgiven through faith in the sacrifice of Jesus.

When Jesus said on the cross, *"It is finished"* (John 19:30), He finished the work of bringing us back to God. Through Jesus, we are no longer enemies of God. Through the cross, Jesus has opened the way so we can come before the throne of God with full confidence to receive His mercy and grace (see Chapter 1). This is the Real Faith.

For All People

Jesus gave His life for the sins of all humanity. He suffered on the cross for people of every nation, language, race, color, social class, caste, and tribe.

John 3:16 can be restated as, God so loved the world—the entire world—that He gave His one and only Son, that whoever—anyone, anywhere in the world—believes in Him shall not perish, but have eternal life.

---

[48] God's holiness.

Chapter 3

John the Baptist was sent as a messenger before Jesus. When he saw Jesus coming toward him, he said, *"Look, the Lamb[49] of God, who takes away the sin of the world!"* (John 1:29). Later, John the disciple wrote: *Jesus Christ, the Righteous One[50]. He is the atoning sacrifice for our sins, and not only for ours but also for the sins of the whole world* (1 John 2:1-2). Salvation through Jesus is available to all, but each individual must make a personal choice.

Conclusion

With the vision of your mind and heart, you can see Jesus on the cross suffering the most intense pain, and giving His life. We should have been the ones dying on that cross. But, Jesus took our place. There was absolutely nothing we could do to have our sins forgiven.

The Real Faith demands accepting the sacrifice made for you. Jesus Christ is the only One who can take your sins away because He paid the penalty for everyone's sins. He has already finished the work on the cross. There is nothing more that remains to be done. Therefore, accept His stretched out hand of peace.

---

[49] In the Holy Scriptures, the lamb is used as a symbol for Jesus as the Sinless One who carried the sins of the world and was slaughtered (crucified) as a sacrifice.

[50] When applied to Jesus, it means the Sinless One.

CHAPTER 4

The Victory

To him who loves us and has freed us from our sins by his blood ... to him be glory and power for ever and ever! Amen" (Revelation 1:5-6).

Jesus rescued us from sin by shedding His blood on the cross. But, the cross was not the end. Jesus gained victory over death once and for all, and He lives for ever and ever.

In His Revelation[51] to John, His beloved disciple, Jesus said, *"I am the Living One; I was dead, and now look, I am alive for ever and ever! And I hold the keys of death and Hades[52]"* (1:18). Jesus overcame death and the grave (return of the dead body to dust or ashes).

After the Cross, the Burial

After Jesus had died on the cross, *as evening approached, there came a rich man from Arimathea, named Joseph, who had himself become a disciple of Jesus. Going to Pilate, he asked for Jesus' body ...* (Matthew 27:57-58). Pilate was surprised to hear that he was

---

[51] Something that is made known.
[52] Grave.

already dead.[53] *Summoning the centurion, he asked him if Jesus had already died. When he learned from the centurion that it was so, he gave the body to Joseph* (Mark 15:44-45). The Roman army officer had already made sure earlier that Jesus was dead when *one of the soldiers pierced Jesus' side with a spear, bringing a sudden flow of blood and water* (John 19:34).

> Joseph of Arimathea *was accompanied by Nicodemus, the man who earlier had visited Jesus at night. Nicodemus brought a mixture of myrrh and aloes, about seventy-five pounds*[54]. *Taking Jesus' body, the two of them wrapped it, with the spices, in strips of linen. This was in accordance with Jewish burial customs. At the place where Jesus was crucified, there was a garden, and in the garden a new tomb, in which no one had ever been laid. ... they laid Jesus there* (19:39–42).

The tomb was a cave cut out of a rock, and a large stone was then rolled to close its mouth. Inside, the cave would have a bench carved out of the rock on which the body would be laid. *The women who had come with Jesus from Galilee followed Joseph and saw the tomb and how his body was laid in it. Then they went home and prepared spices and perfumes* (Luke 23:55-56). The women prepared spices and perfumes to embalm the body of Jesus, as the custom was in those days.

The Tomb—Sealed and Guarded

The chief priests were successful in having Jesus killed. Now, they came up with a plan to keep Him in the tomb.

> *The next day ... the chief priests and the Pharisees went to Pilate. "Sir," they said, "we remember that while he was still alive that deceiver said, 'After three days I will rise again.' So give the order for the tomb to be made*

---

[53] Death on the cross was very slow. It was unusual for someone to die in just 6 hours.
[54] Approximately 34 kilograms.

secure until the third day. Otherwise, his disciples may come and steal the body and tell the people that he has been raised from the dead. This last deception will be worse than the first."

"Take a guard[55]," Pilate answered. "Go, make the tomb as secure as you know how." So they went and made the tomb secure by putting a seal on the stone and posting the guard (Matthew 27:62–66).

Pilate ordered the chief priests to take a guard of soldiers to secure the tomb. A seal was put on the stone so no one could come and open the tomb.

The Open Tomb

Matthew recorded what happened on the third day of the crucifixion:

There was a violent earthquake, for an angel of the Lord came down from heaven and, going to the tomb, rolled back the stone and sat on it. His appearance was like lightning, and his clothes were white as snow. The guards were so afraid of him that they shook and became like dead men (Matthew 28:2–4).

In spite of their best efforts, the chief priests and Pilate were powerless to hold the tomb secure. Absolutely terrified, the guards must have run away to save their lives. Later that morning, the eyewitnesses did not see any guards at the tomb.

Power to Rise Again

Even before His crucifixion, Jesus spoke about laying down His life and taking it up again. *The reason my Father loves me is that I lay down my life—only to take it up again. No one takes it from me, but I lay it down of my own accord. I have authority to lay it down and*

---

[55] A guard of several soldiers. In addition to Roman soldiers, the guard would have included the ones who had been sent by the priests to arrest Jesus in Gethsemane.

authority to take it up again (John 10:17-18). Jesus gave His life voluntarily, otherwise the angels of Heaven were ready to free Him, and no earthly power could have succeeded over the armies of Heaven (see the section, Meaning of the Cross, in Chapter 3).

Jesus had the power to give His life on the cross, and to become alive again. That's why He could say, *"I am the resurrection*[56] *and the life"* (11:25). *It was impossible for death to keep its hold on him* (Acts 2:24).

Jesus had plainly told His disciples that He would die and then rise again. This was shortly after the disciples had understood that Jesus was the Christ, the Son of the living God (see the section, What the Disciples Knew, in Chapter 2). *From that time on Jesus began to explain to his disciples that he must go to Jerusalem and suffer many things at the hands of the elders, the chief priests and the teachers of the law, and that he must be killed and on the third day be raised to life* (Matthew 16:21). This prophecy by Jesus must have reached the ears of the high priests. Very likely it was through Judas who was a disciple of Jesus, but who afterwards betrayed Him and had Him arrested.[57] The chief priests remembered the prediction of Jesus when they asked Pilate to secure the tomb.

The Empty Tomb

Mary Magdalene was the first one to come to the tomb very early in the morning. *Early on the first day of the week,*[58] *while it was still dark, Mary Magdalene went to the tomb and saw that the stone had been removed from the entrance* (John 20:1). Mary must have been a brave woman to go alone to the tomb while it was still dark. She was from the town of Magdala, and had become a follower of Jesus along with several other women.

Mary was baffled and afraid to see that the tomb was open. *So she came running to Simon Peter and the other disciple, the one Jesus*

---

[56] Becoming alive after being dead.

[57] Judas took 30 silver coins from the chief priests, and led the guards to Gethsemane for Jesus' arrest.

[58] Sunday.

loved,[59] and said, *"They have taken the Lord out of the tomb, and we don't know where they have put him!"* (20:2).

At this time, shortly after the crucifixion and burial of Jesus, all His followers were in a state of shock. None of them either remembered or believed that He must rise from the dead.

So, after getting the news of the open tomb from Mary Magdalene, Peter and John started running to the tomb to see what had happened. Both of them looked and went inside the empty tomb. They saw *the strips of linen lying there, as well as the cloth that had been wrapped around Jesus' head. (They still did not understand from Scripture that Jesus had to rise from the dead.)* [20: 6-7, 9].

The Lord Has Risen

Mary Magdalene was quite sure that someone had removed the body of Jesus. That's all she could think about. On her way back from the empty tomb, she joined some other women who were on their way to the tomb with the spices they had prepared to embalm Jesus' body. By this time, it was *just after sunrise* (Mark 16:2):

> *The women took the spices they had prepared and went to the tomb. ... but when they entered, they did not find the body of the Lord Jesus. While they were wondering about this, suddenly two men in clothes that gleamed like lightning stood beside them. In their fright the women bowed down with their faces to the ground, but the men said to them, "Why do you look for the living among the dead? He is not here; he has risen! Remember how he told you, while he was still with you in Galilee: 'The Son of Man must be delivered over to the hands of sinners, be crucified and on the third day be raised again.'" Then they remembered his words* (Luke 24:1, 3–8).

The two men whose clothes gleamed like lightning were angels from Heaven. Because of the brightness of the angels' clothes, the women lowered their heads. While the other women experienced

---

[59] This disciple is identified as John.

meeting the two angels inside the tomb and stayed just long enough to hear the angels' words, Mary Magdalene must have stayed away from the tomb looking for Jesus. The resurrection was the farthest from her thoughts. She was intent on finding out the mystery of the empty tomb on her own.

Meeting angels in their Heavenly glory is a terrifying experience. *Trembling and bewildered, the women went out and fled from the tomb. They said nothing to anyone, because they were afraid* (Mark 16:8). The women left quickly, leaving Mary Magdalene behind while she was looking for Jesus. The women *hurried away from the tomb, afraid yet filled with joy, and ran to tell his disciples. Suddenly Jesus met them. "Greetings," he said. They came to him, clasped his feet and worshiped him. Then Jesus said to them, "Do not be afraid. Go and tell my brothers to go to Galilee; there they will see me"* (Matthew 28:8–10). Jesus is worthy of worship because He is God. Jesus Himself had said, *"Worship the Lord your God and serve him only"* (Luke 4:8). By accepting worship, Jesus proved that He was God.

Left alone near the tomb, Mary Magdalene did not find Jesus. Disappointed, *Mary stood outside the tomb crying* (John 20:11).

> *As she wept, she bent over to look into the tomb and saw two angels in white, seated where Jesus' body had been, one at the head and the other at the foot. They asked her, "Woman, why are you crying?"*
>
> *"They have taken my Lord away," she said, "and I don't know where they have put him." At this, she turned around and saw Jesus standing there, but she did not realize that it was Jesus.*
>
> *He asked her, "Woman, why are you crying? Who is it you are looking for?"*
>
> *Thinking he was the gardener, she said, "Sir, if you have carried him away, tell me where you have put him, and I will get him."*
>
> *Jesus said to her, "Mary."*

She turned toward him and cried out in Aramaic, "Rabboni!" (which means "Teacher") [20:11–16].

Mary fell at the feet of Jesus and held on to Him. Jesus said, *"Do not hold on to me, for I have not yet ascended[60] to the Father"* (20:17).

The Unbelief

The women told their experiences to the disciples. Mary Magdalene even said, *"I have seen the Lord!" And she told them that he had said these things to her* (John 20:18). *But they did not believe the women, because their words seemed to them like nonsense* (Luke 24:11). *Peter, however, got up and ran to the tomb* (24:12). This second time, Peter seems to have gone alone, hoping that he too may see Jesus alive and check out the women's story. But all he saw inside the tomb were *strips of linen lying by themselves, and he went away, wondering to himself what had happened* (24:12).

The Living Christ Appears to Many

So far, the risen Lord had appeared only to the women who had come with Jesus from Galilee, before the crucifixion. Some of these women were Mary Magdalene, Mary the mother of James, and Salome (Mark 16:1), and Joanna (Luke 24:10). But there were also *others with them* (24:10).

Two Travelers Meet Him

We have the following account recorded in Luke 24:13–20:

> *Now that same day two of them were going to a village called Emmaus, about seven miles from Jerusalem. They were talking with each other about everything that had happened. As they talked and discussed these things with each other, Jesus himself came up and walked along with them; but they were kept from recognizing him.*

---

[60] Gone up into heaven.

> *He asked them, "What are you discussing together as you walk along?"*
>
> *They stood still, their faces downcast[61]. One of them, named Cleopas, asked him, "Are you the only one visiting Jerusalem who does not know the things that have happened there in these days?"*
>
> *"What things?" he asked.*
>
> *"About Jesus of Nazareth," they replied. ... "The chief priests and our rulers handed him over to be sentenced to death, and they crucified him ... ."*

Jesus was quite well known in Jerusalem. He had attended the Jewish feasts, and at those occasions, He taught and preached in the temple. He had also healed people in Jerusalem.

Cleopas and his friend were surprised that the person who had joined them did not know about the crucifixion of a well-known man, Jesus. These events had occurred just three days ago, and had become widely known in Jerusalem. Cleopas and his friend continued:

> *"In addition, some of our women amazed us. They went to the tomb early this morning but didn't find his body. They came and told us that they had seen a vision of angels, who said he was alive. Then some of our companions went to the tomb and found it just as the women had said, but they did not see Jesus"* (24:22–24).
>
> Jesus answered them, *"Did not the Messiah have to suffer these things and then enter his glory?" And beginning with Moses and all the Prophets, he explained to them what was said in all the Scriptures concerning himself"* (24:26-27).
>
> *As they approached the village to which they were going, Jesus continued on as if he were going farther. But they*

---

[61] Sad.

urged him strongly, "Stay with us, for it is nearly evening; the day is almost over." So he went in to stay with them.

When he was at the table with them, he took bread, gave thanks, broke it and began to give it to them. Then their eyes were opened and they recognized him, and he disappeared from their sight (24:28–31).

Simon Peter Sees Him

Cleopas and his friend *got up and returned at once to Jerusalem. There they found the Eleven*[62] *and those with them, assembled together and saying, "It is true! The Lord has risen and has appeared to Simon"* (Luke 24:33-34). Before Cleopas and his friend could give the news of Jesus' resurrection to the other followers of Jesus, He had already appeared to Simon Peter. *Then the two told what had happened on the way, and how Jesus was recognized by them when he broke the bread (24:35).*

Among the Disciples

Jesus finally appeared to the other disciples:

While they were still talking about this, Jesus himself stood among them and said to them, "Peace be with you."

They were startled and frightened, thinking they saw a ghost. He said to them, "Why are you troubled, and why do doubts rise in your minds? Look at my hands and my feet. It is I myself! Touch me and see; a ghost does not have flesh and bones, as you see I have."

When he had said this, he showed them his hands and feet. And while they still did not believe it because of joy and amazement, he asked them, "Do you have anything

---

[62] Of the 12 disciples, Judas, the betrayer, had committed suicide. Matthew 27:5: *So Judas threw the money into the temple and left. Then he went away and hanged himself.*

here to eat?" They gave him a piece of broiled fish, and he took it and ate it in their presence (Luke 24:36–43).

By showing them His nail-pierced hands and feet and by eating a piece of fish, Jesus proved to them that He had risen in bodily form.

For the Sake of Thomas

When Jesus appeared to the other disciples, Thomas was not there. So, Jesus appeared again for the sake of Thomas, who had doubted that Jesus was alive.

> *Now Thomas (also known as Didymus), one of the Twelve, was not with the disciples when Jesus came. So the other disciples told him, "We have seen the Lord!"*
>
> *But he said to them, "Unless I see the nail marks in his hands and put my finger where the nails were, and put my hand into his side, I will not believe."*
>
> *A week later his disciples were in the house again, and Thomas was with them. Though the doors were locked, Jesus came and stood among them and said, "Peace be with you!" Then he said to Thomas, "Put your finger here; see my hands. Reach out your hand and put it into my side. Stop doubting and believe."*
>
> *Thomas said to him, "My Lord and my God!"*
>
> *Then Jesus told him, "Because you have seen me, you have believed; blessed are those who have not seen and yet have believed"* (John 20:24–29).

Today, we believe in Jesus because many eyewitnesses have written in the Holy Scriptures about what He did and taught. Jesus calls you blessed when you believe in Him by faith, not having seen Him. Do you believe? If you do, you are blessed.

Chapter 4

Breakfast on the Beach

Jesus once again appeared to the disciples, this time by the Sea of Galilee. The disciples went out to fish and they fished the whole night. *Early in the morning, Jesus stood on the shore, but the disciples did not realize that it was Jesus. When they landed, they saw a fire of burning coals there with fish on it, and some bread. Jesus said to them, "Come and have breakfast." None of the disciples dared ask him, "Who are you?" They knew it was the Lord. Jesus came, took the bread and gave it to them, and did the same with the fish. This was now the third time Jesus appeared to his disciples after he was raised from the dead* (John 21:4, 9, 12–14).

Other Appearances

Jesus appeared to many others *over a period of forty days*, and He *gave many convincing proofs that he was alive* (Acts 1:3). The apostle Paul, who had obtained personal reports from Jesus' disciples, wrote: *He appeared to Cephas,*[63] *and then to the Twelve. After that, he appeared to more than five hundred of the brothers and sisters at the same time ..."* (1 Corinthians 15:5-6).

Seen in Visions

One of the most dramatic appearances of the living Christ was in a vision to Saul of Tarsus, who later became known as the apostle Paul. Saul had become quite famous for hating and persecuting[64] the early believers in Jesus.

> *Saul was still breathing out murderous threats against the Lord's disciples. He went to the high priest and asked him for letters to the synagogues*[65] *in Damascus, so that if he found any there who belonged to the Way,*[66] *whether men*

---

[63] Peter's Aramaic name.
[64] To persecute: To bully and mistreat the followers of Jesus.
[65] Jewish places of worship and assembly.
[66] The faith practiced by the early followers of Jesus was known as The Way. Because of their mistreatment by the Jews in Jerusalem, many of these early followers of Jesus had settled in Damascus, Syria.

or women, he might take them as prisoners to Jerusalem. As he neared Damascus on his journey, suddenly a light from heaven flashed around him. He fell to the ground and heard a voice say to him, "Saul, Saul, why do you persecute me?"

"Who are you, Lord?" Saul asked.

"I am Jesus, whom you are persecuting," he replied. "Now get up and go into the city, and you will be told what you must do."

The men traveling with Saul stood there speechless; they heard the sound but did not see anyone. Saul got up from the ground, but when he opened his eyes he could see nothing. So they led him by the hand into Damascus (Acts 9:1–8).

In a vision, the Lord spoke about Saul to a disciple named Ananias, saying, *"Go! This man is my chosen instrument to proclaim my name to the Gentiles*[67] *and their kings and to the people of Israel"* (9:15). Ananias went to see Saul. When he placed his hands on Saul, *immediately, something like scales fell from Saul's eyes, and he could see again. He got up and was baptized …* (9:18). Later, Saul came to be known as Paul, who became a great apostle of Jesus Christ. The conversion of Saul is a clear example of a life changed by Jesus. Paul later gave his life for the sake of Jesus Christ.

Meaning of the Resurrection

The resurrection of Jesus was a real event. He did not turn into a ghost. He rose from the dead in bodily form. He is alive today, and He lives for ever and ever.

Jesus is the only One who left behind an empty tomb after His death and burial. A number of men who started their own religions, such as Buddha, Krishna, Mohammed, Nanak, and a few others, came and died. No one ever claimed that any of them rose from the dead; and they are certainly not alive today. A claim

---

[67] Non-Jews.

Chapter 4

about the resurrection has been made only for Jesus, because it is true. Several hundred eyewitnesses saw Him after His resurrection in bodily form.

The Real Faith is firmly based on the resurrection of Jesus Christ. The apostle Paul wrote: *If Christ has not been raised, our preaching is useless and so is your faith* (1 Corinthians 15:14). If Jesus would not have risen from the dead, then His death on the cross would have been useless and meaningless, because *if Christ has not been raised, your faith is futile; you are still in your sins* (15:17). Therefore, if Jesus had not risen from the dead, then the entire world would be lost in sin, without any hope.

The resurrection of Jesus gives us assurance of two things: (1) If we ask Him to forgive our sins, we can be certain that our sins are forgiven, and (2) all those who have died believing in Jesus will rise from the dead. *In Christ all will be made alive* (1 Corinthians 15:22). This is explained further in Chapter 9.

Return to Heaven

Forty days after the resurrection, Jesus met with His disciples on the Mount of Olives. There, Jesus *lifted up his hands and blessed them. While he was blessing them, he left them and was taken up into heaven* (Luke 24:50-51). *He was taken up before their very eyes, and a cloud hid him from their sight. They were looking intently up into the sky as he was going, when suddenly two men dressed in white*[68] *stood beside them. "Men of Galilee," they said, "why do you stand here looking into the sky? This same Jesus, who has been taken from you into heaven, will come back in the same way you have seen him go into heaven"* (Acts 1:9–11).

Jesus ascended into Heaven in the presence of His followers. *Then the apostles returned to Jerusalem from the hill called the Mount of Olives ...* (1:12). The two angels said that this same Jesus—the One who was crucified and then rose from the dead—will come back again in the same way as He was seen ascending into Heaven. The return of Jesus is covered in Chapter 9.

---

[68] These two men in white were angels from Heaven.

High Priest in Heaven

In the ancient Jewish temple in Jerusalem, the high priest used to sacrifice animals—such as lambs, goats, and bulls—for the sins of the people. Jesus was the symbol of an innocent sacrificial lamb. *After he had provided purification for sins* (Hebrews 1:3) by His death on the cross, *he sat down at the right hand of the Majesty in heaven* (1:3) after His resurrection and return to Heaven. His sacrifice on the cross once and for all finished the need for animal sacrifices. Jesus has become the High Priest in Heaven: *We do have such a high priest, who sat down at the right hand of the throne of the Majesty in heaven* (8:1). *Therefore he is able to save completely those who come to God through him, because he always lives to intercede*[69] *for them* (7:25). Jesus became *a merciful and faithful high priest in service to God ... that he might make atonement*[70] *for the sins of the people* (2:17). By His death, resurrection, and ascension[71] to Heaven, Jesus is able to save completely anyone who comes to God through Him. The apostle Paul wrote: *Now in Christ Jesus you who once were far away have been brought near by the blood of Christ* (Ephesians 2:13). Sin had removed us far from God, but now by what Jesus has done, anyone can come before the throne of God.

Conclusion

It was essential for Jesus to rise from the dead and ascend to Heaven to complete the work of salvation. He is the only One who can save us completely. His victory is our victory when we believe in Him.

Therefore, since we have a great high priest who has ascended into heaven, Jesus the Son of God, let us hold firmly to the faith we profess (Hebrews 4:14). You must profess your faith in the One and only Savior. That is the Real Faith.

---

[69] To take our side before God.
[70] Forgiveness and removal of sin by Jesus.
[71] The return of Jesus to Heaven.

CHAPTER 5

What Must I Do?

Sin is like a deadly disease that has infected humanity. Sin leads to destruction—total and complete destruction. *All sinners will be destroyed ...* (Psalms 37:38). One choice we all have is to continue to live a life of sin. A person can *enjoy the fleeting pleasures of sin* (Hebrews 11:25) for a short time. But, if the person continues in sin, the end of it will be destruction. A better choice that we also have is to find salvation and eternal life in Jesus Christ. *For the wages of sin is death, but the gift of God is eternal life in Christ Jesus our Lord* (Romans 6:23).

The Human Cry

Jesus had now returned to Heaven. On the day of Pentecost,[72] Jerusalem was filled with many visitors from various countries. *Then Peter stood up with the Eleven, raised his voice and addressed the crowd* (Acts 2:14). In his message, Peter explained that Jesus was crucified and raised from the dead according to God's plan of salvation. Peter used the words of David who was a prophet:

---

[72] A Jewish feast, also known as the Feast of Weeks. It came 50 days after the Passover.

> *"Seeing what was to come, he spoke of the resurrection of the Messiah, that he was not abandoned to the realm of the dead,[73] nor did his body see decay. God has raised this Jesus to life, and we are all witnesses of it"* (2:31-32).

Peter further explained that Jesus had been *exalted to the right hand of God* (2:33), which had fulfilled another prophecy given by David. Then Peter said, *"God has made this Jesus, whom you crucified, both Lord and Messiah"* (2:36). When the people heard this, they were cut to the heart and said to Peter and the other apostles, *"Brothers, what shall we do?"* (2:37).

At another time, Paul and his missionary[74] companion, Silas, were in a foreign city called Philippi. The Roman citizens in this city brought false charges against them and had them put in prison.

> *About midnight Paul and Silas were praying and singing hymns to God, and the other prisoners were listening to them. Suddenly there was such a violent earthquake that the foundations of the prison were shaken. At once all the prison doors flew open, and everyone's chains came loose. The jailer[75] called for lights, rushed in and fell trembling before Paul and Silas. He then brought them out and asked, "Sirs, what must I do to be saved?"* (16:25-26, 29-30).

Millions of people around the world are trying to find out what they must do to receive forgiveness. They turn to religion, ceremonies and rituals, prayers in shrines, journeys to "holy" places, and chants and mantras, but they fail to receive the assurance of forgiveness and salvation. In their hearts, they keep asking the same old question: "What must I do to receive forgiveness?" "Have I done enough?" "Do I need to do more?" "What else can I do?" Before you finish this chapter, you will have the answer to

---

[73] The grave.
[74] One who is sent out to share the message of Jesus with others.
[75] The one in charge of the prison.

these questions. You may be someone who has learned religious teachings. You may have gone through certain rituals. You may have religion; but, have you found salvation? You need to be sure.

The Message

John the Baptist, son of Zechariah, prepared the way for the ministry of Jesus. John was preaching and saying, *"Repent, for the kingdom of heaven has come near"* (Matthew 3:2). *People went out to him from Jerusalem and all Judea and the whole region of the Jordan*[76]. *Confessing their sins, they were baptized by him in the Jordan River* (3:5-6).

After John was put in prison, Jesus went into Galilee, proclaiming the good news of God. *"The time has come,"* he said. *"The kingdom of God has come near. Repent and believe the good news!"* (Mark 1:14-15). On the day of Pentecost, when the crowd asked the question, *"What shall we do?"* Peter replied, *"Repent and be baptized, every one of you, in the name of Jesus Christ for the forgiveness of your sins"* (Acts 2:37-38).

The central message preached by John the Baptist, Jesus, and the apostles was to repent. The answer to the question, "What must I do?" has four steps.

Step One: Believe

In their response to the jailer's cry in Philippi, Paul and Silas said, *"Believe in the Lord Jesus, and you will be saved—you and your household"* (Acts 16:31). So, the first step is to believe in the Lord Jesus. Peter's message created a stir in people's hearts after they had believed in the crucifixion, resurrection, and ascension of Jesus Christ.

At this point, if you are not quite sure about who Jesus is, why He gave His life on the cross, and why He was raised to life and returned to Heaven, then please go back and reread Chapters 2, 3, and 4.

---

[76] The main river in Israel.

Do you now believe that Jesus is God, and that He came to this Earth in human form as the Son of God? John, the beloved disciple, wrote: *This is how you can recognize the Spirit of God: Every spirit that acknowledges that Jesus Christ has come in the flesh is from God, but every spirit that does not acknowledge Jesus is not from God* (1 John 4:2-3). Believing that Jesus Christ has come in the flesh requires a firm belief in four things: (1) Jesus was God who *became flesh and made his dwelling among us* (John 1:14); (2) He took our sins upon Himself, and paid the full penalty for our sins on the cross; (3) He is both Lord and Christ because He rose from the dead and ascended to Heaven; and (4) He is our High Priest at the right hand of God the Father, offering complete forgiveness of our sins.

Step Two: Repent

Repent by coming to the throne of grace in prayer. Repentance[77] begins with a humble heart. To illustrate how we should come to the throne of God, Jesus told this parable:

> "Two men went up to the temple to pray, one a Pharisee and the other a tax collector. The Pharisee stood by himself and prayed: 'God, I thank you that I am not like other people ... or even like this tax collector. I fast twice a week and give a tenth of all I get.'
>
> "But the tax collector stood at a distance. He would not even look up to heaven, but beat his breast and said, 'God, have mercy on me, a sinner.'
>
> "I tell you that this man, rather than the other, went home justified[78] before God. For all those who exalt themselves will be humbled, and those who humble themselves will be exalted" (Luke 18:10–14).

---

[77] Confession of sins to God with humility, and turning away from past sinful ways.
[78] Accepted and forgiven.

Chapter 5

Pride is what keeps many people from repenting. People who think they are too good and do not need to repent fail to receive God's forgiveness. Others hold high positions, and they worry what their friends and peers would think. Still others are like the Pharisee in the story Jesus told. They think that they have religion, and have no need to repent. But, salvation cannot be obtained without repentance. Repentance includes five main things:

1. Come to God in total humility.

    The prophet Joel wrote: *"Even now,"* declares the LORD, *"return to me with all your heart, with fasting and weeping and mourning." Rend your heart and not your garments* (Joel 2:12-13). Even King David came to God with great humility. He wrote: *My sacrifice, O God, is a broken spirit; a broken and contrite heart you, God, will not despise* (Psalms 51:17). A contrite heart feels deeply sorry and remorseful before God.

2. Confess[79] your sins.

    If we claim we have not sinned, we make him out to be a liar and his word is not in us (1 John 1:10), *and we deceive ourselves and the truth is not in us* (1:8). Own up your sins to God. Sins should be confessed to God alone.

3. Believe that Jesus gave His life on the cross for your sins.

    Trust that your sins have been forgiven. *The blood of Jesus, his Son, purifies us from all sin. If we confess our sins, he is faithful and just and will forgive us our sins and purify us from all unrighteousness*[80] (1 John 1:7, 9). The blood of Jesus purifies us from every type of sin and every type of wrongdoing.

4. Forgive other people.

    Jesus taught us to pray: *"Forgive us our sins, for we also forgive everyone who sins against us"* (Luke 11:4). He Himself set the

---

[79] Own up before God.
[80] Sinfulness.

example for us when, at the time of His crucifixion, He prayed, *"Father, forgive them, for they do not know what they are doing"* (23:34).

5. Turn around, change, and give up sinning.

Repent, then, and turn to God, so that your sins may be wiped out ... (Acts 3:19). Through true repentance, God wipes out our sins. When God forgives, our record of sin no longer exists. It is as if we got a clean white page under our name. After receiving forgiveness, *no one who is born of God will continue to sin* (1 John 3:9).

Step Three: Open the Door

Revelation 3:19-20 paints a picture of Jesus standing at the door and knocking. He stands at the door of your heart, but He does not force His way in. You must open the door and invite Him in:

"Those whom I love I rebuke and discipline. So be earnest and repent. Here I am! I stand at the door and knock. If anyone hears my voice and opens the door, I will come in and eat with that person, and they with me."

In another beautiful Scripture, Jesus said:

"Anyone who loves me will obey my teaching. My Father will love them, and we will come to them and make our home with them" (John 14:23).

We cannot help but love Jesus with eternal gratitude for what He has done for us. When we open the door of our heart to invite Him in, He makes a wonderful promise: both He and the Father come into our heart and they make their home with us. God living in us; what else can we hope for?

Step Four: Receive Baptism

Before ascending to Heaven, Jesus commanded His disciples to *go and make disciples of all nations, baptizing them in the name of the Father and of the Son and of the Holy Spirit ...* (Matthew 28:19).

Chapter 5

To set an example, Jesus Himself was baptized by John, son of Zechariah, even though He did not need baptism:

Then Jesus came from Galilee to the Jordan to be baptized by John. But John tried to deter him, saying, "I need to be baptized by you, and do you come to me?"

Jesus replied, "Let it be so now; it is proper for us to do this to fulfill all righteousnes." Then John consented. As soon as Jesus was baptized, he went up out of the water (3:13–16).

Baptism is a holy rite. It seals the steps of righteousness discussed here—having faith in the completed work of the Lord Jesus Christ, repenting of sins, and inviting Jesus into our hearts. Baptism is also a public expression of a person's faith in Jesus. The holy rite of baptism in water is a means of expressing faith in the death, burial, and resurrection of Jesus Christ:

Don't you know that all of us who were baptized into Christ Jesus were baptized into his death? We were therefore buried with him through baptism into death in order that, just as Christ was raised from the dead through the glory of the Father, we too may live a new life (Romans 6:3-4).

Baptism is a commitment to God.[81] The new believer commits to living a new and changed life by God's help.

Like a Child

Once Jesus was with His disciples when He *called a little child to him, and placed the child among them. And he said: "Truly I tell you, unless you change and become like little children, you will never enter the kingdom of heaven"* (Matthew 18:2-3). Repentance requires a change in attitude. It requires coming to God without personal

---

[81] In rare circumstances, due to severe illness or disability, a person may not be able to receive baptism. Repentance and faith in Christ still assure his/her salvation.

pride and pretense. It requires total trust in God, just like a child trusts its parents.

Born of God

After repentance and baptism, a believer in Jesus starts a new life. The apostles Paul and Timothy wrote: *The old has gone, the new is here! All this is from God, who reconciled us to himself through Christ ... not counting people's sins against them* (2 Corinthians 5:17–19).

Nicodemus, a religious leader, had come to talk to Jesus one night. Jesus knew what was on his mind. So, straightaway Jesus said to him, *"Very truly I tell you, no one can see the kingdom of God unless they are born again. No one can enter the kingdom of God unless they are born of water and the Spirit"* (John 3:3, 5).

Speaking of Jesus, John the beloved disciple wrote: *To all who did receive him, to those who believed in his name, he gave the right to become children of God ... born of God* (1:12-13). A person who has accepted Christ by faith and repentance and is baptized is born anew, born of God, in a spiritual sense. True repentance and baptism make a person *receive the gift of the Holy Spirit* (Acts 2:38). Hence, such a person is born of water (through baptism) and the Spirit.

The experience of being born again is also called "conversion." Regardless of background and upbringing, or status in life, every single person must be converted to enter God's kingdom. Nicodemus was a very religious man, but Jesus told him that he needed to be born again.

Now Is the Time

It is natural to make plans for this life, but it is often done while neglecting one's salvation. As a result, many have become rich in this life, but have remained poor toward God. Jesus once told a story to a crowd of people:

> "The ground of a certain rich man yielded an abundant harvest. He thought to himself, 'What shall I do? I have no place to store my crops.'

Chapter 5

"Then he said, 'This is what I'll do. I will tear down my barns and build bigger ones, and there I will store my surplus grain. And I'll say to myself, "You have plenty of grain laid up for many years. Take life easy; eat, drink and be merry."'

"But God said to him, 'You fool! This very night your life will be demanded from you. Then who will get what you have prepared for yourself?'

"This is how it will be with whoever stores up things for themselves but is not rich toward God" (Luke 12:16–21).

Are you ready to make a commitment to God? God speaks to people through the Holy Scriptures and through His Spirit. *Today, if you hear his voice, do not harden your hearts* (Hebrews 3:15). The prophet Jeremiah wrote about the condition of people who reject God's offer of mercy. A time will come when they will say, *"The harvest is past, the summer has ended, and we are not saved"* (Jeremiah 8:20). *Now is the time of God's favor, now is the day of salvation* (2 Corinthians 6:2). The prophet Isaiah wrote: *Seek the LORD while he may be found; call on him while he is near* (Isaiah 55:6).

People of all ages need to receive the salvation that only Christ can offer. To the young people, the wise man says, *"Remember your Creator in the days of your youth, before the days of trouble come and the years approach when you will say, 'I find no pleasure in them'"* (Ecclesiastes 12:1). Young people face many temptations; they want to be like their peers. They feel pressured to do what their peers do. As time passes, the attractions of this world choke the desire to turn one's life over to Christ. So, if you are a young person, you will be infinitely better off going through your life with God than without Him.

To the older folks, the wise man says, *"Remember him—before the silver cord is severed, and the golden bowl is broken ... and the dust returns to the ground it came from ..."* (12:6-7). Older people also face temptations, perhaps of a different kind than younger people do. They also must turn their lives over to Christ before it is too late.

If at one time you had accepted Christ as your savior, but have since turned away, you can come back to Him while He still waits for you. If you have never accepted Him as your savior before, He waits for you too. What is keeping you back? Even now, you can go to a quiet place and give your heart to God through a simple prayer:

> "Lord Jesus, come into my heart. I believe that you died in my place on the cross. Forgive my sins. Give me the new life that you have promised. Make me your own and become the Lord of my life. Help me to obey you. Thank you, Jesus. Amen."

Conclusion

Everyone is in need of repentance. You may be religious; you may know the doctrines[82]; you may even understand salvation intellectually. But, Jesus said that you must be born again, otherwise you cannot even see the kingdom of God. A person who is born anew by receiving Jesus becomes a child of God—*To all who did receive him, to those who believed in his name, he gave the right to become children of God* (John 1:12). The child of God has a new life.

---

[82] Religious teachings.

CHAPTER 6

The New Life

True repentance results in a new life marked by devotion, trust, fellowship, obedience, sharing, and peace. God forgave our sins. We did not deserve it, but we received forgiveness because of His grace.

> *For it is by grace you have been saved, through faith—and this is not from yourselves, it is the gift of God—not by works, so that no one can boast* (Ephesians 2:8).

Salvation is a free gift from God. It is received when a person accepts by faith Jesus Christ as Lord and Savior through repentance, as discussed in the previous chapter. This is the Real Faith that brings with it a new way of living. The Real Faith is a lifelong journey with Christ.

> *If anyone is in Christ, the new creation has come: The old has gone, the new is here!* (2 Corinthians 5:17).

The new life is lived in harmony with God's will. This is because our salvation has been purchased at a great price:

> *You are not your own; you were bought at a price* (1 Corinthians 6:19-20). *It was not with perishable things*

such as silver or gold that you were redeemed[83] from the empty way of life handed down to you from your ancestors, but with the precious blood of Christ ... (1 Peter 1:18-19).

A born-again believer's life belongs to God. He rescued it from destruction at a great price—the precious blood of Christ. Even a normal life, without Christ, is empty.

For the lifelong journey with Christ, God has promised:

"I know the plans I have for you ... plans to prosper you and not to harm you, plans to give you hope and a future. Then you will call on me and come and pray to me, and I will listen to you" (Jeremiah 29:11-12).

God has also said, *"Do not fear, for I am with you; do not be dismayed[84], for I am your God. I will strengthen you and help you; I will uphold you with my righteous[85] right hand* (Isaiah 41:10).

Jesus made a personal promise to His followers: *"Surely I am with you always, to the very end of the age[86]"* (Matthew 28:20).

Devotional Life

Devotion to God includes study of the Holy Scriptures, prayer, fasting, thanksgiving, and praise. For a new believer, these things may not all come at once. It is fine to grow into them slowly at your own pace.

---

[83] Forgiven and delivered from sin by accepting the sacrifice of Jesus on the cross.

[84] Discouraged.

[85] Holy.

[86] A time when the present era will come to an end. The last stage of this earth's history.

Chapter 6

Study

The Holy Scriptures ... are able to make you wise for salvation through faith in Christ Jesus (2 Timothy 3:15). Regular study of the Holy Scriptures is essential, because it strengthens a person's faith in God.

God does not have a chosen language. Either the entire Holy Bible or the New Testament is available in almost all major languages of the world.[87] If you have never read the Bible, start with the New Testament. Let the Holy Spirit guide you even though you may not understand everything. A slow, thoughtful, prayerful study can help you understand many things that will enrich your life.

Prayer

We come to the throne of God in prayer. There is no one set prayer. True prayer is not something made up and repeated over and over. Jesus said, *"When you pray, do not keep on babbling like pagans[88], for they think they will be heard because of their many words"* (Matthew 6:7).

We should present our requests to God when we pray, and we should bring our requests with thanksgiving. The apostles Paul and Timothy wrote: *Do not be anxious about anything, but in every situation, by prayer and petition, with thanksgiving, present your requests to God* (Philippians 4:6).

Jesus also warned, *"When you pray, do not be like the hypocrites, for they love ... to be seen by others. ... But when you pray, go into your room, close the door and pray to your Father, who is unseen. Then your Father, who sees what is done in secret, will reward you"* (Matthew 6:5-6).

Prayers do not need any special words or some set formula. A prayer coming from a person's heart, in the name of Jesus, brings

---

[87] The complete Bible is available in more than 500 languages. The New Testament is available in another 1,300 languages. The Scriptures are also available online for free.

[88] People who do not believe in the one true God found in the Holy Scriptures.

that person into the very presence of God. Jesus said, *"I will do whatever you ask in my name ...* (John 14:13). The believer can open his/her heart to God without fear. In the name of Jesus, we can *approach God's throne of grace with confidence, so that we may receive mercy and find grace to help us ...* (Hebrews 4:16).

Among the teachings of Jesus is what has come to be known as the Lord's Prayer. It is a pattern that we can follow when we pray. It is recorded in Matthew 6:9–13 (NKJV)[89]:

> *Our Father in heaven,*
> *Hallowed[90] be Your name.*
> *Your kingdom come.*
> *Your will be done*
> *On earth as it is in heaven.*
> *Give us this day our daily bread.*
> *And forgive us our debts,*
> *As we forgive our debtors.*
> *And do not lead us into temptation,*
> *But deliver us from the evil one.*
> *For Yours is the kingdom and*
> *the power and the glory forever.*
> *Amen.*

When we accept Jesus, the Ruler of the Universe becomes "our God" and "our Father in heaven" in a very personal way. You can address Him as "my God" and "my Father." When we come to Him in humble prayer, He does not turn us away. The born-again believer forms a special bond with God. God loved us first, and we can love Him in return, just like the songwriter who declared, *"I love the LORD ..."* (Psalms 116:1).

We come to God with the understanding that His name is holy. So, we must remember that we are in the presence of a holy God. We can ask Him to purify our hearts and minds.

---

[89] Scripture taken from the New King James Version®. Copyright © 1982 by Thomas Nelson, Inc. Used by permission. All rights reserved.
[90] Holy.

Chapter 6

The Lord's Prayer reminds us that one day God's kingdom will be established on this Earth (more about the kingdom is discussed in Chapter 8). This is what John heard in the Revelation given to him: *The kingdom of the world has become the kingdom of our Lord and of his Messiah, and he will reign[91] for ever and ever* (Revelation 11:15). All the redeemed[92] will rule with Jesus in His kingdom. So, believers should be in a right relationship with God, doing everything that the new life requires.

We should pray for God's will to be done on this Earth and in our lives. First and foremost, it is God's will that no one should perish. *He is patient with you, not wanting anyone to perish, but everyone to come to repentance* (2 Peter 3:9). When we have received salvation through Jesus Christ, we should pray for the salvation of others. God's will is found in the Holy Scriptures. *Do not merely listen to the word, and so deceive yourselves. Do what it says* (James 1:22). For God's will to be done in our lives, we should ask for His guidance in doing what the Scriptures say. But when He guides us, we should also be willing to follow His leading. He often closes one door as He opens another. We need to be patient as He fulfills His will in our lives.

Daily bread is both physical and spiritual. God provides for our physical needs. We should daily thank Him for it. We should also ask Him for spiritual guidance as we read the Holy Scriptures and come to Him in prayer.

The biggest debt that God forgives is the debt of sin. *As far as the east is from the west, so far has he removed our transgressions from us* (Psalms 103:12). When we are forgiven, God makes a beautiful promise: *I, even I, am he who blots out your transgressions ... and remembers your sins no more* (Isaiah 43:25). God says that He not only forgives, He erases the record of our sins, and He does not remember those sins any more. Wow! There is just one thing that even God will forget—our sins that have been forgiven.

---

[91] Rule.
[92] Those who are forgiven and delivered from sin by accepting the sacrifice of Jesus on the cross.

So, just as God forgives us so completely, we also must forgive others. Peter once asked Jesus, *"Lord, how many times shall I forgive my brother or sister who sins against me? Up to seven times?" Jesus answered, "I tell you, not seven times, but seventy-seven times"* (Matthew 18:21-22). God expects us to be kind and merciful just as He is. That's why Jesus said, *"If you do not forgive others their sins, your Father will not forgive your sins"* (6:15).

We should pray that when temptations come our way, God will keep us from falling. The word for "temptation" in the original language is also translated as "trial" or "test." A person who is truly converted will go through many trials and temptations in his/her life. But you must always remember: *No temptation has overtaken you except what is common to mankind. And God is faithful; he will not let you be tempted beyond what you can bear. But when you are tempted, he will also provide a way out so that you can endure it* (1 Corinthians 10:13). Prayer is needed more than ever before when we must go through trials and temptations.

God allows trials in our lives to strengthen our faith, but trials and temptations are brought by the evil one, who is also called Satan and Devil—the enemy of mankind (this enemy is unmasked in Chapter 10). God is able to deliver us from the hands of the enemy.

No matter what happens, God gives us the assurance of His Heavenly kingdom. *The Lord will rescue me from every evil attack and will bring me safely to his heavenly kingdom. To him be glory for ever and ever. Amen* (2 Timothy 4:18). We should believe these assuring words.

The apostles Paul, Silas, and Timothy advised us to *pray continually* (1 Thessalonians 5:17). We can say a prayer from our heart anytime, anywhere—we can pray while walking, talking to someone, or driving a car. Then, we must also make time for heartfelt prayers in a formal way, when we are alone with God.

> *Jesus told his disciples a parable to show them that they should always pray and not give up. He said: "In a certain town there was a judge who neither feared God nor cared*

what people thought. And there was a widow in that town who kept coming to him with the plea, 'Grant me justice against my adversary[93].'

"For some time he refused. But finally he said to himself, 'Even though I don't fear God or care what people think, yet because this widow keeps bothering me, I will see that she gets justice, so that she won't eventually come and attack me!'"

And the Lord said, "Listen to what the unjust judge says. And will not God bring about justice for his chosen ones, who cry to him day and night? Will he keep putting them off?" (Luke 18:1–7).

Then the Lord added, *"I tell you, he will see that they get justice, and quickly"* (18:8).

We don't know when and how God will answer our prayers. The above story teaches that we should not lose heart or give up. Rather, we should continue praying. God answers prayers in His own ways, according to His plans and purposes. We simply need to trust Him.

Fasting

There is no particular time, month, or season for fasting. Fasting fits in with other acts of devotion to God. In other words, fasting should accompany study of the Scriptures, prayer, thanksgiving, and praise. Otherwise, fasting alone is meaningless. Fasting is particularly useful when we have a great need to come to God for His mercy and grace. Fasting helps create an attitude of humility before God. It gives us a greater degree of faith when we come to Him.

Here are just three examples: Before starting His ministry, Jesus fasted to overcome the devil's temptations.[94] Queen Esther

---

[93] Enemy.
[94] Recorded in Matthew 4:1–11.

announced a fast to save her people from the evil schemes of an enemy.[95] The apostles fasted and prayed before taking up some important task in God's service.[96]

This is what Jesus taught about fasting:

> *"When you fast, do not look somber as the hypocrites do, for they disfigure their faces to show others they are fasting. Truly I tell you, they have received their reward in full. But when you fast, put oil on your head and wash your face, so that it will not be obvious to others that you are fasting, but only to your Father, who is unseen; and your Father, who sees what is done in secret, will reward you"* (Matthew 6:16–18).

Thanksgiving

Being thankful is an ongoing attitude that goes hand in hand with prayer and praise. The songwriter wrote: *Let us come before him with thanksgiving and extol*[97] *him with music and song. For the LORD is the great God, the great King above all gods* (Psalms 95:2-3).

We should come to God with thankful hearts. We should thank God in whatever we do. *Whatever you do, whether in word or deed, do it all in the name of the Lord Jesus, giving thanks to God the Father through him* (Colossians 3:17). We should thank God in every situation. *Rejoice always, pray continually, give thanks in all circumstances; for this is God's will for you in Christ Jesus* (1 Thessalonians 5:16–18). At all times, our hearts should overflow with joy, prayer, and thanksgiving when we are born anew and living the new life. When we are living the Real Faith, even undesirable circumstances are for our benefit and for the glory of God, even though we may not fully understand them.

---

[95] Recorded in Esther 4:15–17.
[96] Recorded in Acts 13:3 and 14:23.
[97] Praise and worship.

Chapter 6

Praise

Praise, thanksgiving, and worship go hand in hand. Praise can be in word, song, or music. The Psalms are full of praise and thanksgiving to God. For example, the psalmist[98] has written:

> It is good to praise the LORD and make music to your name, O Most High (Psalms 92:1).
>
> Shout for joy to the LORD, all the earth. Worship the LORD with gladness; come before him with joyful songs.
>
> Enter his gates with thanksgiving and his courts with praise; give thanks to him and praise his name.
>
> For the LORD is good and his love endures forever; his faithfulness continues through all generations (100:1-2, 4-5).

Trust in God

Trusting God for everything is a key element of the Real Faith. The book of Proverbs is full of wise sayings. About trust, it says: *Trust in the LORD with all your heart and lean not on your own understanding; in all your ways submit to him, and he will make your paths straight* (Proverbs 3:5-6). Why should we trust God, instead of trusting our own understanding? Here is the answer: *The foolishness of God is wiser than human wisdom, and the weakness of God is stronger than human strength* (1 Corinthians 1:25).

Jesus once asked the question, *"Which of you fathers, if your son asks for a fish, will give him a snake instead? Or if he asks for an egg, will give him a scorpion?"* (Luke 11:11-12). If our earthly parents can give us good things, how much more we should trust our Heavenly Father to meet all our needs. Jesus talked about trust in God by using the examples of simple needs we all have:

> Jesus said to his disciples: "Therefore I tell you, do not worry about your life, what you will eat; or about your body, what you will wear. For life is more than food, and

---

[98] Songwriter.

the body more than clothes. Consider the ravens: They do not sow or reap, they have no storeroom or barn; yet God feeds them. And how much more valuable you are than birds!" (12:22–24).

"Consider how the wild flowers grow. They do not labor or spin. Yet I tell you, not even Solomon in all his splendor was dressed like one of these. If that is how God clothes the grass of the field, which is here today, and tomorrow is thrown into the fire, how much more will he clothe you—you of little faith! And do not set your heart on what you will eat or drink; do not worry about it. For the pagan world runs after all such things, and your Father knows that you need them. But seek his kingdom, and these things will be given to you as well" (12:27–31).

Trusting God establishes a special relationship between God and us. *The LORD is good, a refuge in times of trouble. He cares for those who trust in him* (Nahum 1:7). This verse can also be translated as: He knows those who trust in him. As we trust God, and He fulfills our needs, we get to know Him better. We can trust God with full confidence. *Those who know your name trust in you, for you, LORD, have never forsaken those who seek you* (Psalms 9:10).

Fellowship

Born-again believers should first and foremost have fellowship with God through study of the Holy Scriptures, prayer, fasting, thanksgiving, praise, and trust. But fellowship with other believers is an important aspect of growing and advancing in the Real Faith. Jesus said, *"Where two or three gather in my name, there am I with them"* (Matthew 18:20). So, fellowship with believers includes fellowship with Christ.

Fellowship with other believers does not necessarily mean joining an established church congregation. Other than formal membership in a church, you may participate in a men's fellowship group, a women's fellowship group, or a youth group. You may even start a neighborhood fellowship group or participate in one where neighbors regularly meet for study, prayer, and praise.

Obedience

The Real Faith requires obedience to God. We do not obey God to receive His pardon. Rather, we obey Him because He has pardoned us and has given us the priceless gift of salvation.

In the works Jesus did when He was on this Earth, He healed people of various diseases and infirmities. Healing and forgiveness of sins went hand in hand. And, Jesus warned those who were healed to not sin anymore. For example, Jesus once healed a man who had been very sick for 38 years. He then warned this man, *"See, you are well again. Stop sinning or something worse may happen to you"* (John 5:14).

Jesus said, *"If you love me, keep my commands"* (John 14:15). Obedience follows when we personally come to know the loving God that He is. John, the beloved disciple, wrote: *We know that we have come to know him if we keep his commands. Whoever says, "I know him," but does not do what he commands is a liar, and the truth is not in that person. But if anyone obeys his word, love for God is truly made complete in them* (1 John 2:3–5). Love for God and obedience to His commands go hand in hand.

Disobedience to God is sin. *Everyone who sins breaks the law; in fact, sin is lawlessness* (1 John 3:4). Here we have a definition of what sin is: it is acting against God's law. God's law for all time is contained in the Ten Commandments. So, sin is disobeying any of the Ten Commandments.

Here is a question for us who have been saved by God's grace: *Shall we go on sinning so that grace may increase?* (Romans 6:1). Our answer must be: *By no means!* (6:2). *No one who is born of God will continue to sin, because God's seed remains in them; they cannot go on sinning, because they have been born of God* (1 John 3:9). In the new life, there is no room for sinful habits.

Is One Sinner Worse Than Another?

One day Jesus was teaching a large crowd. Some came and told Him about the people from Galilee who were put to death by Pilate (the same Roman governor who crucified Jesus).

> *Jesus answered, "Do you think that these Galileans were worse sinners than all the other Galileans because they suffered this way? I tell you, no! But unless you repent, you too will all perish. Or those eighteen who died when the tower in Siloam fell on them—do you think they were more guilty than all the others living in Jerusalem? I tell you, no! But unless you repent, you too will all perish"* (Luke 13:2–5).

When the people came to Jesus and mentioned the fate of the Galileans killed by Pilate, Jesus knew what they were thinking—that people who face tragedies in their lives are worse sinners than others. Jesus said, "No." He then gave another example of people who died in an accident when part of a tower broke off and fell on them. They too were not worse sinners than others. More importantly, twice Jesus made the statement, *"But unless you repent, you too will all perish"* (13:3; 13:5). People often repent and turn to God when tragedies strike. When life is going well, it is easy to ignore the need for repentance.

Confession, repentance, and forsaking of sin follow each other. *Whoever conceals their sins does not prosper, but the one who confesses and renounces*[99] *them finds mercy* (Proverbs 28:13).

Does the new life mean that sin will never again enter our thoughts or deeds? No, it does not mean that. Sometimes, we may stumble and fall. Then, what do we do? In his old age, John the beloved disciple wrote, *"My dear children, I write this to you so that you will not sin. But if anybody does sin, we have an advocate*[100] *with*

---

[99] To renounce: to turn away from.

[100] Jesus, our High Priest in heaven (see page 54), brings us back to God when we confess our sins to Him.

the Father—Jesus Christ, the Righteous One. He is the atoning sacrifice for our sins ..." (1 John 2:1-2).

God's Law

In Romans 3:20 we read: *Through the law we become conscious of our sin,* which is also translated as: "Through law is full knowledge of sin."[101] We come to understand what sin is by paying attention to the law given by God.

The Ten Commandments were written by God Himself. *When the LORD finished speaking to Moses on Mount Sinai, he gave him the two tablets of the covenant law*[102], *the tablets of stone inscribed by the finger of God* (Exodus 31:18). Deuteronomy 10:4 clarifies what the covenant law, written on the tablets, is: *The LORD wrote on these tablets what he had written before, the Ten Commandments ... .*

God made a covenant—a deal—with humans that they will obey Him. God gave the tablets of the Ten Commandments to Moses, the man chosen by God. Moses recorded the Ten Commandments for all of us. Apart from God's law, no other record on Earth tells people what sin is.

To obey or not to obey is a person's choice; but God has made one thing clear, when He said, *"See, I am setting before you today a blessing*[103] *and a curse*[104]*—the blessing if you obey the commands of the LORD your God ... the curse if you disobey the commands of the LORD your God and turn from the way that I command you today by following other gods ..."* (Deuteronomy 11:26–28).

The Ten Commandments

Following is a summary of the Ten Commandments, found in Exodus 20:1–17:

---

[101] *The Interlinear Greek-English New Testament.* The Nestle Greek Text with a Literal English Translation by the Reverend Alfred Marshall. Second Edition. Grand Rapids, Michigan: Zondervan Publishing House, 1958.

[102] The law of Ten Commandments that establishes God's relationship with us and our relationship with Him.

[103] God's gifts to us.

[104] God's curse brings destruction.

1. *"I am the LORD your God ... . You shall have no other gods before me"* (20:2-3).

   The LORD is the one and only true God. He Himself has declared, *"I am the LORD, and there is no other; apart from me there is no God"* (Isaiah 45:5).

   God has made Himself known in the person of Jesus Christ. We can know the one and only true God in only one way—through and in Jesus Christ. In Hebrews 1:3, we read: *The Son is the radiance of God's glory and the exact representation of his being. In Christ all the fullness of the Deity lives in bodily form* (Colossians 2:9). *God was pleased to have all his fullness dwell in him* (1:19). It is very clear that apart from Christ, God cannot be known. All other systems of trying to know God only lead to finding false gods.

2. *"You shall not make for yourself an image*[105] *... . You shall not bow down to them or worship them ..."* (Exodus 20:4).

   Worship of images, idols, and statues is common in many parts of the world. It does not matter what or who the images and idols represent; bowing down to them and worshiping them is sin. God is not a thing; He does not live in any thing. Therefore, do not bow down to anything.

   Some examples of things that people worship include idols and images that are *formed like a man or a woman ... any animal ... any bird ... any creature that moves along the ground or any fish ...* (Deuteronomy 4:16–18). Further, God said, *"And when you look up to the sky and see the sun, the moon and the stars ... do not be enticed into bowing down to them ..."* (4:19). In some cultures, other human beings—alive or dead—are worshiped. This too is worship of idols.

3. *"You shall not misuse the name of the LORD your God, for the LORD will not hold anyone guiltless*[106] *who misuses his name"* (Exodus 20:7).

---

[105] Idol or picture.
[106] Sinless.

Chapter 6

This commandment refers to the wrongful use of the name of God. His name is holy and is reserved for holy use. Some of the correct ways in which we use God's name are in prayer, praise, and giving of thanks. Some of the wrong ways include use of God's name in bad language and swearing. The name of Jesus is also to be reserved for holy use. We read: *At the name of Jesus every knee should bow, in heaven and on earth ... and every tongue acknowledge that Jesus Christ is Lord, to the glory of God the Father* (Philippians 2:10-11). Even the careless use of expressions such as, "O God," or "O Jesus," amount to sin unless the expressions are used seriously in prayer, praise, or thanksgiving.

4. *"Remember the Sabbath day by keeping it holy. The seventh day is a sabbath to the LORD your God"* (Exodus 20:8, 10).

   God said to remember, because most people have forgotten or neglected to keep the Sabbath day holy.

5. *"Honor your father and your mother ..."* (20:12).

   God commands us to respect our parents. Youngsters must obey their parents. The apostle Paul wrote: *Children, obey your parents in the Lord, for this is right. "Honor your father and mother"—which is the first commandment with a promise—"so that it may go well with you and that you may enjoy long life on the earth"* (Ephesians 6:1–3). Paul then goes a step further, and places a responsibility on the parents also: *Fathers, do not exasperate[107] your children; instead, bring them up in the training and instruction of the Lord* (6:4).

6. *"You shall not murder"* (Exodus 20:13).

   Violence against and killing of innocent people are taking place in many parts of the world. In some countries and cultures, violence and killings are being carried out in the

---

[107] Make angry; make mad.

name of the gods that these people follow. God, however, wrote very plainly with His own finger, "You shall not kill another person."

God is the giver of life. He does not give any person the right to take human life that He has created. All life is sacred in God's eyes, because Jesus gave His life on the cross for the salvation of every human being. Referring to the devil, Jesus once said, *"He was a murderer from the beginning ..."* (John 8:44). So, the devil is the author of all types of murders and killings. In other words, those who kill needlessly are following the devil.

7. *"You shall not commit adultery"* (Exodus 20:14).

This is a warning against all types of immorality, in thought or deed.

8. *"You shall not steal"* (20:15).

God says, "Do not take and keep without permission what does not belong to you."

9. *"You shall not bear false testimony against your neighbor"* (20:16).

Any kind of lie or deceit is sin. *The LORD detests lying lips ...* (Proverbs 12:22). Therefore, *a false witness will not go unpunished, and whoever pours out lies will perish* (19:9). Talking about the devil, Jesus said, *"He is a liar and the father of lies"* (John 8:44). So, lying and deception are characteristics of the devil.

10. *"You shall not covet ..."* (Exodus 20:17).

This commandment is a warning against envy and greed. As a general rule, it means not to desire what others have. Whatever you do have is given to you by God. So, be content with it and be thankful to Him.

Chapter 6

Many cultures and religions of the world, in one form or another, have accepted some of the Ten Commandments. But, no religion on Earth accepts all 10 of them. Only in the Real Faith do we understand that all the Ten Commandments must be obeyed. Breaking any one of these commands is sin. *For whoever keeps the whole law and yet stumbles at just one point is guilty of breaking all of it* (James 2:10).

Are Certain Sins Less Serious Than Others?

In the eyes of God, sin is sin. One sin is no worse than another. This means that we should guard ourselves and pray that we will not sin even in matters that may appear small to us. We may think that certain sins—such as lying, deceit, and greed—can't be too serious. Here is an account described in 2 Kings 5:1–27:

> *Now Naaman was commander of the army of the king of Aram[108]. ... He was a valiant soldier, but he had leprosy[109]* (5:1).
>
> A Hebrew slave girl told Naaman's wife, *"If only my master would see the prophet who is in Samaria! He would cure him of his leprosy"* (5:3).

So Naaman traveled to Israel, taking with him sizable treasures. Once in Israel, he was directed to see the prophet Elisha.

> *So Naaman went with his horses and chariots and stopped at the door of Elisha's house* (5:9). But, *Elisha sent a messenger to say to him, "Go, wash yourself seven times in the Jordan, and your flesh will be restored and you will be cleansed"* (5:10).

Namaan was disappointed that the prophet did not even come out to meet him. He had expected that the prophet would put his hand on him to cure him.

---

[108] Syria, as referenced in Luke 4:27.
[109] A terrible skin disease that often eats into the flesh.

> Naaman's servants reasoned with him and said, *"If the prophet had told you to do some great thing, would you not have done it? How much more, then, when he tells you, 'Wash and be cleansed'!"* (5:13).

Naaman took the advice of his servants. He went down to the Jordan River, dipped in it seven times, and was fully cured of his disease.

To show his gratitude, Naaman returned to Elisha's house and tried to offer him gifts from his treasures. But the prophet refused to take any gifts. Then, it so happened!

> *After Naaman had traveled some distance, Gehazi, the servant of Elisha the man of God, said to himself, "My master was too easy on Naaman, this Aramean, by not accepting from him what he brought." ... So Gehazi hurried after Naaman* (5:19–21).

> *Catching up with Naaman down the road, Gehazi said, "My master sent me to say, 'Two young men from the company of the prophets have just come to me ... . Please give them a talent[110] of silver and two sets of clothing'"* (5:22).

Out of his generosity, Naaman gave not one but two talents of silver and clothing, and asked two of his servants to carry them.

> *When Gehazi came to the hill, he took the things from the servants and put them away in the house. He sent the men away and they left* (5:24).

> *Elisha asked him, "Where have you been, Gehazi?" "Your servant didn't go anywhere," Gehazi answered* (5:25).

> *But Elisha said to him, "Was not my spirit with you when the man got down from his chariot to meet you? Is this the time to take money or to accept clothes ... ? Naaman's leprosy will cling to you and to your descendants forever."*

---

[110] About 75 pounds (34 kilograms). It was a large sum of money.

Chapter 6

> *Then Gehazi went from Elisha's presence and his skin was leprous ...* (5:26-27).

Gehazi was greedy. He thought that as an Israelite he was entitled to Naaman's money, because Naaman was a foreigner. To get the money and clothes, Gehazi told Naaman a lie. He was also sneaky and deceptive. Before reaching home, he took the gifts from Naaman's servants and quietly brought them into the house. He again told a lie to Elisha when asked where he had been.

Gehazi had to face terrible results for sins that did not appear too serious to him. But, what if he had confessed his sins and repented before God? We can be sure that his sins would have been forgiven, and he would have avoided the dreadful disease from touching him and his children.

Sharing

The last message Jesus gave before returning to Heaven was about sharing—sharing your Real Faith with others. On the Mount of Olives, Jesus said to His disciples, *"You will be my witnesses in Jerusalem, and in all Judea and Samaria, and to the ends of the earth"* (Acts 1:8). According to Jesus' prophecy about the end of this age, the *gospel*[111] *of the kingdom will be preached in the whole world as a testimony to all nations, and then the end will come* (Matthew 24:14). [More details are given in Chapter 15].

Followers of Christ must share the Gospel with others. Jesus left the glories of heaven to come to this world of sin, hatred, and violence. He gave His all to save us. We must ask ourselves, "What are we doing for Him?"

But, what is the Gospel that we must share? By reading this book thus far, you have actually read the Gospel message.

Although the word "gospel" means "good news," it is a unique message. The Gospel message that John the Baptist, our Lord Jesus, and the apostles preached was about salvation through the grace of Jesus Christ. Salvation is absolutely essential to enter into

---

[111] The message of salvation through the grace of Jesus Christ.

the kingdom of God. Salvation cannot be received by our own works—we can never do enough good to receive salvation. The good news is that Jesus has paid the penalty for our sins—all sins—so we can be free from the condemnation of sin and have eternal life. The good news is that the blood of Jesus guarantees salvation. This is the message that everyone in the world must hear.

We should never be ashamed of the Gospel of the Lord Jesus Christ. The apostle Paul wrote: *I am not ashamed of the gospel, because it is the power of God that brings salvation to everyone who believes* (Roman 1:16). Through the Gospel, the power of God brings salvation to all who believe. Hence, the message of the Gospel must go out to everyone. *Whoever believes and is baptized will be saved, but whoever does not believe will be condemned* (Mark 16:16).

Jesus once rescued a man from demons, and gave him a new life. He then told the man, "*Return home and tell how much God has done for you*" (Luke 8:39). He was asked to share that it was Jesus who had given him a new life, so that others would be drawn to Jesus.

The apostle Peter has given some good advice on how to share the message of salvation: *In your hearts revere[112] Christ as Lord. Always be prepared to give an answer to everyone who asks you to give the reason for the hope that you have. But do this with gentleness and respect* (1 Peter 3:15). Sharing is not about arguing with people. Before someone can ask you about why you have the assurance of salvation, you must share with them the hope and assurance that you have. And then explain to them the way of salvation with gentleness and respect. Do not put down other people, or their religion. Pressure and hostility are not the tactics Jesus or His apostles used. Share with people that Christ is the only way to salvation, and explain why that is so. At the right moment, facts can be presented in a tactful way, without compromise, to make people think. They still may not accept the message of the Gospel; but that's their choice.

---

[112] Worship.

Chapter 6

Be at Peace

Jesus once assured his disciples, *"Peace I leave with you; my peace I give you"* (John 14:27). The born-again believer receives the inner peace that only God can give. In turn, He commands His followers to be at peace with others: *If it is possible, as far as it depends on you, live at peace with everyone. Do not take revenge ... but leave room for God's wrath, for it is written: "It is mine to avenge; I will repay," says the Lord* (Romans 12:18-19). If others do not want to live in peace with you, the only thing you can do is to pray that they too will find salvation and peace through Jesus Christ. Jesus gave this command: *"Pray for those who persecute you, that you may be children of your Father in heaven"* (Matthew 5:44-45). When someone does us wrong, it is a natural human tendency to try and get even. But, the command is: *Do not take revenge ... "I will repay," says the Lord* (Romans 12:19). So, leave it to God, fully believing that He will take revenge in His own way and in His own time.

Conclusion

This chapter covers a number of important things about how to live the new life in Christ once you have received His gift of salvation. It may well require reading more than once. The new life is lived with the help of the Holy Spirit. This theme is explained in the next chapter.

CHAPTER 7

The Divine Companion

The Holy Spirit is a person of the Godhead—the Deity or the God family (about the God family, see the section, The LORD is One, in Chapter 2). The Holy Spirit was present with all who were appointed by God for a special work. For example, David—who was a king and a prophet—once pleaded with God, *"Do not cast me from your presence or take your Holy Spirit from me"* (Psalms 51:11).

The Holy Spirit was also present with Jesus when He was on this Earth. As described in Chapter 5, Jesus received baptism from John, the son of Zechariah—also called, John the Baptist—to set an example for us. Luke recorded: *When all the people were being baptized, Jesus was baptized too. And as he was praying, heaven was opened and the Holy Spirit descended on him in bodily form like a dove. And a voice came from heaven: "You are my Son, whom I love; with you I am well pleased"* (Luke 3:21-22). Soon after His baptism, *Jesus, full of the Holy Spirit, left the Jordan and was led by the Spirit into the wilderness ...* (4:1).

After Jesus returned to Heaven, the Holy Spirit became the divine Companion of Jesus' followers. In the same way, the Holy

Spirit becomes a constant Companion for the believer who continues to live the new life discussed in the previous chapter.

The One God

The Godhead has three members—it is one Family of three persons—the Father, the Son (whom we know as Jesus Christ), and the Holy Spirit. These three are one in perfect unity. References to them are found in both the Old and the New Testaments of the Holy Scriptures, leaving no doubt that the Deity has three persons. The knowledge that the Deity comprises three distinct persons who are in perfect unity is absolutely essential for a correct understanding of the Holy Scriptures.

Notice that in a passage in the Old Testament, the LORD (the Father), the Savior (Jesus, who redeemed His people), and the Holy Spirit (who is grieved by people's sins) are named separately. Yet, they appear to be one and the same in the narrative, which shows perfect unity among the three:

> *I will tell of the kindness of the LORD, the deeds for which he is to be praised ... .*
>
> *He said, "Surely they are my people, children who will be true to me"; and so he became their Savior.*
>
> *In his love and mercy he redeemed them ... . Yet they rebelled and grieved his Holy Spirit* (Isaiah 63:7, 8–10).

A few days before Jesus returned to Heaven after His resurrection, He had asked His disciples to meet Him on a mountain in Galilee. Jesus had a special command to give them:

> *When they saw him, they worshiped him; but some doubted. Then Jesus came to them and said, "All authority in heaven and on earth has been given to me. Therefore go and make disciples of all nations, baptizing them in the name of the Father and of the Son and of the Holy Spirit, and teaching them to obey everything I have*

> *commanded you. And surely I am with you always, to the very end of the age"* (Matthew 28:17–20).

Of particular note in the above Scripture is the fact that the One Name includes the Father, the Son, and the Holy Spirit. As the Scripture in Luke 3:21-22 (cited earlier) informs us, at the baptism of Jesus, the Holy Spirit descended on Him and the Father's voice came from Heaven, saying, *"You are my Son, whom I love; with you I am well pleased"* (3:22). We find that the Father, the Son, and the Holy Spirit, though distinct, are present together. In his final greeting to the believers in Corinth, the apostle Paul wrote: *May the grace of the Lord Jesus Christ, and the love of God, and the fellowship of the Holy Spirit be with you all* (2 Corinthians 13:14). We see again that the three persons are mentioned together. The grace of Jesus Christ, the love of God the Father, and the fellowship of the Holy Spirit will continue to work in the lives of the believers till the end of time.

The Spirit's Work in Salvation

It is through the Holy Spirit that a person becomes convicted of sin. The Spirit gently leads that person to repentance and faith in Jesus Christ that bring salvation. Such a person is born anew through the leading of the Holy Spirit.

> In Titus 3:4-5 we read: *When the kindness and love of God our Savior appeared, he saved us, not because of righteous things we had done, but because of his mercy. He saved us through the washing of rebirth and renewal by the Holy Spirit.*

Spiritual rebirth and the new life are experienced when a person responds to the gentle tug of the Holy Spirit on the heart, and accepts Jesus Christ as savior. The gentle tug, or the gentle whisper of the Holy Spirit, can be easily ignored. Repentance and salvation become impossible for those who constantly put off the gentle promptings of the Holy Spirit. That's why it says: *Today, if you hear his voice, do not harden your hearts ...* (Hebrews 3:15).

The Divine Companion

At the Passover supper, before Jesus and His disciples went to Gethsemane, Jesus had a discussion with His disciples. In just a few more hours Jesus was going to be arrested and falsely condemned, as pointed out in Chapter 3. Jesus had told His disciples very plainly, *"One of you is going to betray me"* (John 13:21). Then He said, *"I will be with you only a little longer"* (13:33). On hearing these words, the disciples had become very sad. So, Jesus encouraged them with the promise of the Holy Spirit. He said, *"I will not leave you as orphans; I will come to you"* (14:18). Again, Jesus said, *"You heard me say, 'I am going away and I am coming back to you'"* (14:28).

How would Jesus come to be with His disciples after He went back to Heaven? How would He keep His promise, *"Surely I am with you always, to the very end of the age"* (Matthew 28:20)?

This is what Jesus said: *"I will ask the Father, and he will give you another advocate to help you and be with you forever—the Spirit of truth"* (John 14:16-17). Jesus further explained, *"It is for your good that I am going away. Unless I go away, the Advocate will not come to you; but if I go, I will send him to you"* (16:7). In the original language, the word translated as "advocate" means "someone who has been called to a person's side." Hence, it is also translated as "helper" or "comforter." But, the main sense of the word can also refer to a Companion—someone who is with a person to help and guide. The Holy Spirit helps and guides a believer throughout the life's journey.

More importantly, this Companion is divine; He is the third person of the Deity. The presence of the Holy Spirit is exactly as if Jesus Himself were with us. Indeed, by the Holy Spirit, both the Father and the Son dwell with the believer. This is what Jesus said, *"Anyone who loves me will obey my teaching. My Father will love them, and we will come to them and make our home with them"*

(14:23). The Father too spoke through the prophet Isaiah: *This is what the high and exalted One says—he who lives forever, whose name is holy: "I live in a high and holy place, but also with the one who is contrite and lowly in spirit ..."* (Isaiah 57:15). In the person of the Holy Spirit, God lives with the one who humbles himself/herself before God, repents of all sins, and accepts Jesus Christ.

Why the Companion

The new life described in Chapter 6 is a life of victory over sin. This life of victory can be lived only with the help of the Holy Spirit. This section explains how a person receives the companionship of the Holy Spirit, and the ways in which the Holy Spirit helps a believer.

Receiving the Divine Companion

There are two main points here: (1) When people asked *Peter and the other apostles, "Brothers, what shall we do?" Peter replied, "Repent and be baptized, every one of you, in the name of Jesus Christ for the forgiveness of your sins. And you will receive the gift of the Holy Spirit* (Acts 2:37-38). So, the Holy Spirit is a gift from God, given to those whose sins have been forgiven through faith in Jesus Christ, as explained in Chapter 5. (2) The Holy Spirit is received through prayer. In His teaching on prayer, Jesus said, *"If you then, though you are evil, know how to give good gifts to your children, how much more will your Father in heaven give the Holy Spirit to those who ask him!"* (Luke 11:13). Jesus has promised, *"Ask and it will be given to you ... . For everyone who asks receives ..."* (11:9-10).

Have your sins been forgiven? Have you received baptism? If so, have you asked God to give you the Holy Spirit in the name of Jesus?

Benefits of Companionship

The Holy Spirit helps us grow in the Real Faith. He shows us the straight way in which we must walk. We have not been left alone as orphans, as Jesus promised. Companionship of the Spirit brings five very important benefits:

First, *The Spirit himself testifies with our spirit that we are God's children* (Romans 8:16). The Holy Spirit gives us the assurance that we are God's children. *Those who are led by the Spirit of God are the children of God* (8:14). It is by Him, the Holy Spirit, that we call God *Abba*[113], *Father* (8:15). There should be no question in the mind of a born-again believer that God is our Father. Jesus also introduced Him to us as *our Father* (Matthew 6:9). The assurance of being God's children carries with it the assurance of salvation. This unshakable assurance is the foundation of the Real Faith.

Second, the Holy Spirit helps us approach the throne of God in prayer. *The Spirit helps us in our weakness. We do not know what we ought to pray for, but the Spirit himself intercedes*[114] *for us through wordless groans. ... the Spirit intercedes for God's people in accordance with the will of God* (Romans 8:26-27). How many times we do not know what to pray for or how to pray for something or someone? What words to use? We can be sure that the Holy Spirit takes our requests and presents them to God in harmony with His will. The Holy Spirit gives us the confidence and the boldness to approach the throne of God without fear.

Third, *no one can say, "Jesus is Lord," except by the Holy Spirit* (1 Corinthians 12:3). It is with the help of the Holy Spirit that we accept Jesus as the Lord and Master of our life. Talking about the Holy Spirit, Jesus said, *"He will glorify me because it is from me that he will receive what he will make known to you"* (John 16:14). The Holy Spirit glorifies Jesus in our lives so we can love Him and obey His commands, as He said, *"If you love me, keep my commands"* (14:15).

Fourth, the Spirit enables us to do God's will. To the believers living in Colossae, the apostles Paul and Timothy wrote: *We continually ask God to fill you with the knowledge of his will through all the wisdom and understanding that the Spirit gives, so that you*

---

[113] Aramaic word for father.
[114] Takes our requests to God.

may live a life worthy of the Lord and please him in every way ... (Colossians 1:9-10). The Holy Spirit gives wisdom and understanding so that the believer can live a life that pleases the Lord.

Fifth, the Holy Spirit gives us the assurance that we have eternal life. Jesus and His disciples were once passing through a town in Samaria, called Sychar. At about noon, tired from His journey, Jesus sat down by a well while the disciples went into town to buy food. Jesus got into a conversation with a woman who came to the well to draw water. Jesus explained to her, *"Everyone who drinks this water will be thirsty again, but whoever drinks the water I give them will never thirst. Indeed, the water I give them will become in them a spring of water welling up to eternal life"* (John 4:13-14). Here, Jesus was talking about the *living water* (4:10)—the Holy Spirit—that only He could give.

Conclusion

The Holy Spirit is a member of the Deity—One with the Father and the Son. He leads men and women to recognize sin in their lives, and leads them to repentance and faith in Jesus Christ. With the help of the Holy Spirit, a person can be spiritually *born of God* (John 1:13). Such a person is given the assurance that he or she is a child of God, and has eternal life. The Holy Spirit is the divine Companion for those born of God. They can call God their Father. They love Jesus, make Him the Lord of their lives, and keep His commands. With the help of the Holy Spirit, they live a new life that glorifies Jesus Christ.

CHAPTER 8

The Kingdom

Both John the Baptist and Jesus emphasized repentance for the forgiveness of sins, but they also linked their message of repentance with the kingdom of God, also called kingdom of Heaven. For example, Matthew recorded: *In those days John the Baptist came, preaching in the wilderness of Judea and saying, "Repent, for the kingdom of heaven has come near"* (Matthew 3:1-2). Similarly, after fasting for 40 days in the wilderness, Jesus came to Galilee where he began His public ministry. He too *began to preach, "Repent, for the kingdom of heaven has come near"* (4:17). Hence, there is a close relationship between salvation that comes through repentance and the kingdom of Heaven. Salvation makes you a citizen of the kingdom of God.

After Jesus returned to Heaven, the apostles preached the same message that Jesus had preached about repentance and the kingdom of God. For example, during his last days, the apostle Paul lived in Rome. *For two whole years Paul stayed there in his own rented house and welcomed all who came to see him. He proclaimed the kingdom of God and taught about the Lord Jesus Christ—with all boldness and without hindrance!* (Acts 28:30-31).

The Holy Scriptures have many references to the kingdom of God. The kingdom refers to both the citizens of the kingdom as well as a physical Heavenly kingdom.

The Divine King

The idea of a kingdom indicates that there is a king. During His trial before Pilate, the Roman governor, one of the accusations the Jewish leaders had brought against Jesus was that He had claimed *to be Messiah, a king* (Luke 23:2). *So Pilate asked Jesus, "Are you the king of the Jews?" "You have said so," Jesus replied* (23:3).

Jesus then continued, *"My kingdom is not of this world. ... But now my kingdom is from another place"* (John 18:36). Jesus did not dispute that He was a king, but He made it clear that His kingdom was not of this world. His kingdom was not like other kingdoms on Earth, and He was not an earthly king.

Before His crucifixion, when Jesus was questioned by the chief priests and the Jewish council, He said, *"But from now on, the Son of Man will be seated at the right hand of the mighty God"* (Luke 22:69). After He rose from the dead, Jesus *was taken up into heaven and he sat at the right hand of God* (Mark 16:19). Today, Jesus sits with the Father on His throne in Heaven.

John, the beloved disciple, was shown a future vision of Jesus. He describes that *on his robe and on his thigh he has this name written: KING OF KINGS AND LORD OF LORDS* (Revelation 19:16). The same title of *King of kings and Lord of lords* is also used for God the Father (1 Timothy 6:15). The Father, the Son, and the Holy Spirit together share the kingship of the universe.

The Kingdom Now

Once the Pharisees asked Jesus *when the kingdom of God would come* (Luke 17:20). *Jesus replied, "The coming of the kingdom of God is not something that can be observed, nor will people say, 'Here it is,' or 'There it is,' because the kingdom of God is in your midst"* (17:20-21). Indeed, the kingdom of God was in the people's midst. First,

Chapter 8

Jesus Himself represented the kingdom of God. He was the Divine King, living in the midst of the people and doing among them the works of God—healing the sick, curing the disabled, raising the dead, and casting out demons. Second, the believers in Jesus—those who have been born of God (see Chapter 5)—are the citizens of the kingdom of God. To the believers in Colossae, the apostles wrote: God *has rescued us from the dominion of darkness and brought us into the kingdom of the Son he loves, in whom we have redemption*[115]*, the forgiveness of sins* (Colossians 1:13-14). The followers of Jesus are in His kingdom, because they have chosen to be under the lordship or kingship of Jesus Christ. To the believers at Philippi, Paul and Timothy wrote: *Our citizenship is in heaven* (Philippians 3:20), that is, the kingdom of Heaven.

Jesus told a number of parables about the kingdom of God. In one of these parables, He used the illustration of seeds—that good seeds produce crops that are used as food, and bad seeds produce weeds. While explaining this parable to His disciples, Jesus said, *"The one who sowed the good seed is the Son of Man. The field is the world, and the good seed stands for the people of the kingdom"* (Matthew 13:37-38). In this parable, Jesus is the sower of the good seed through His teachings. Those who accept and follow His teachings become the citizens of His kingdom.

In two other parables, Jesus used the illustration of a seed to draw lessons about the kingdom of God. In one of these parables, Jesus compared the kingdom of Heaven to a tiny seed that can grow and become a tree:

> *"The kingdom of heaven is like a mustard seed, which a man took and planted in his field. Though it is the smallest of all seeds, yet when it grows, it is the largest of garden plants and becomes a tree, so that the birds come and perch in its branches"* (13:31-32).

---

[115] Forgiveness and deliverance from sin accomplished by Jesus for all those who believe in Him.

When put in the soil, the seed first grows into a plant. Then it keeps on growing till it becomes a tree. First, it illustrates that a believer must continue to grow in the new life, described in Chapter 6. Second, through personal spiritual growth and by sharing the Gospel with others, the kingdom of God continues to grow, as others are brought into the kingdom. The expanding kingdom of God also benefits people all over the world. This happens as individual believers support various Gospel-based organizations that go out into many corners of the world to relieve pain and suffering, following the example of Jesus.

The third "seed parable" is even better known than the previous two. In this parable, a farmer sows seed that falls on four different types of ground, and each produces different results:

> While teaching a large crowd of people, Jesus said, *"A farmer went out to sow his seed. As he was scattering the seed, some fell along the path, and the birds came and ate it up. Some fell on rocky places, where it did not have much soil. It sprang up quickly, because the soil was shallow. But when the sun came up, the plants were scorched, and they withered because they had no root. Other seed fell among thorns, which grew up and choked the plants. Still other seed fell on good soil, where it produced a crop—a hundred, sixty or thirty times what was sown"* (13:3–8).

The disciples did not understand the meaning of this parable. So, they asked Jesus to explain it.

> Jesus said to them, *"Listen then to what the parable of the sower means: When anyone hears the message about the kingdom and does not understand it, the evil one comes and snatches away what was sown in their heart. This is the seed sown along the path. The seed falling on rocky ground refers to someone who hears the word and at once receives it with joy. But since they have no root, they last only a short time. When trouble or*

Chapter 8

persecution[116] *comes because of the word, they quickly fall away. The seed falling among the thorns refers to someone who hears the word, but the worries of this life and the deceitfulness of wealth choke the word, making it unfruitful. But the seed falling on good soil refers to someone who hears the word and understands it. This is the one who produces a crop, yielding a hundred, sixty or thirty times what was sown"* (13:18–23).

In this parable, Jesus explains that there are four types of people who hear or read the message of the Gospel, which is represented by the seed. Clearly, the message of the Gospel does not take root and bear fruit in all people. And such people never become citizens of the kingdom of God. Jesus gave reasons why this is so.

People in the first category, represented by the pathway, do not quite pay attention to the Gospel message. They do not think about it seriously, and so it has no effect on them. They have in fact hardened their hearts against the gentle voice of the Holy Spirit. It is as if the birds came and snatched away the Gospel message. That's why one must respond to the gentle tug of the Holy Spirit, and not put it off.

People in the second category, represented by the rocky ground, receive the message with joy at first. They may even repent and decide to follow Jesus. Their intentions may be good. But, as soon as they have to face some hardship, they quickly give up and turn their backs on Jesus and His Gospel. This happens because they do not continue in earnest to live the new life described in Chapter 6. They too fail to enter the kingdom of God.

People in the third category, represented by the thorny bushes, remain believers in name only. They may participate in religious activities, but the kingdom of God does not become a priority with them. The cares of this life and a constant pursuit of financial success prevent them from entering the kingdom of Heaven. Others may

---

[116] Mistreatment of the followers of Jesus by unbelievers.

achieve financial success, but they do not live the new life of surrender to Jesus Christ. They selfishly keep God's blessings for themselves. They do not take the command of Jesus too seriously: *"Store up for yourselves treasures in heaven ..."* (Matthew 6:20). Someone has fittingly described such attitude by suggesting that such people give a tithe[117] or more to the waitress when they eat in a restaurant, but toss just a tip at God. Every born-again individual has a responsibility to support the ministries that help the poor, and others that take the Gospel message of God's kingdom to the world. This is as much a part of the Real Faith as life's journey in other spiritual matters. But, many fail to enter the kingdom of God because money is more important to them than salvation of others. Yet, God has made a promise of abundant blessing: *"Bring the whole tithe into the storehouse... . Test me in this,"* says the LORD Almighty, *"and see if I will not throw open the floodgates of heaven and pour out so much blessing that there will not be room enough to store it"* (Malachi 3:10). This is not a "get rich quick" scheme. But, God has made a promise of wonderful blessings to the givers. Are you ready to believe it?

People in the fourth category, represented by the good soil, have become citizens of the kingdom. They continue to live the new life and keep the Real Faith regardless of circumstances. Sometimes, circumstances are not as we would like them to be. But, through good times and bad, living the Real Faith produces a harvest for the kingdom of God.

The Future Kingdom

The kingdom of God is also a physical Heavenly kingdom that will be established in the future. That's why in the Lord's Prayer, Jesus taught us to pray: *your kingdom come* (Matthew 6:10). Who will enter into and experience this kingdom? Those who already are citizens of the kingdom now, and they will spend eternity in the kingdom of God.

---

[117] One-tenth.

Chapter 8

Not long before His crucifixion, Jesus was discussing the end of the age with His disciples. In a parable He used in the discussion, Jesus said:

> "When the Son of Man comes in his glory, and all the angels with him, he will sit on his glorious throne. All the nations will be gathered before him, and he will separate the people one from another as a shepherd separates the sheep from the goats. He will put the sheep on his right and the goats on his left.
>
> "Then the King will say to those on his right, 'Come, you who are blessed by my Father; take your inheritance, the kingdom prepared for you since the creation of the world'" (25: 31–34).

In this parable, Jesus used the illustration of sheep and goats, representing two groups of people. One group will enter the kingdom of God, the other will not.

Without End

Many passages of Scripture inform us about the future kingdom of God, which will be ruled by Jesus. The author of the book of Hebrews quotes Psalm 45:6, in which God the Father says this about Jesus: *"Your throne, O God, will last for ever and ever; a scepter of justice will be the scepter of your kingdom"* (Hebrews 1:8). The kingdom of God will never come to an end; it will last for ever and ever. Another prophecy about the government over which Jesus will preside is given by Isaiah in this poetic passage:

> *To us a child is born, to us a son is given,*
> *and the government will be on his shoulders* (Isaiah 9:6).
>
> *Of the greatness of his government and peace there will be no end.*
>
> *He will reign on David's throne and over his kingdom,*

establishing and upholding it with justice and righteousness from that time on and forever (9:7).

In a vision, John the beloved disciple heard *loud voices in heaven, which said,*

> "The kingdom of the world has become
> the kingdom of our Lord and of his Messiah,
> and he will reign for ever and ever" (Revelation 11:15).

While announcing the birth of Jesus to the Virgin Mary, the angel Gabriel said,

> "You will conceive and give birth to a son, and you are to call him Jesus. He will be great and will be called the Son of the Most High. The Lord God will give him the throne of his father David ... his kingdom will never end" (Luke 1:31–33).

The prophet Daniel saw a vision one night and wrote about it:

> "In my vision at night I looked, and there before me was one like a son of man, coming with the clouds of heaven. He approached the Ancient of Days and was led into his presence. He was given authority, glory and sovereign power; all nations and peoples of every language worshiped him. His dominion is an everlasting dominion that will not pass away, and his kingdom is one that will never be destroyed" (Daniel 7:13-14).

Daniel saw this vision and recorded it more than 550 years before the birth of Jesus. He saw someone like a son of man (Jesus) coming to the Ancient of Days (the Father) to receive authority, glory, power, and dominion. Jesus is given dominion over God's kingdom which will last forever.

The above passages of Scripture, from both the Old and New Testaments, make it absolutely clear that (1) Jesus is God, because people of all nations and languages worship Him, (2) the Father turns over the kingdom to Jesus, and (3) as King, Jesus reigns for ever and ever, without end.

Rule with Him

In the same vision cited above, Daniel also saw and wrote:

> "The holy people of the Most High will receive the kingdom and will possess it forever—yes, for ever and ever" (Daniel 7:18).

The holy people are all those who have been saved by the grace of Jesus Christ. For example, the apostle Paul begins his first letter to the believers in Corinth by stating: *To the church of God in Corinth, to those sanctified*[118] *in Christ Jesus and called to be his holy people* ... (1 Corinthians 1:2). Those who believe in Christ and live the new life are referred to as "holy people" or "saints." By living the new life with the help of the Holy Spirit, the saints live a life of victory over sin. According to Daniel's prophecy, they receive the kingdom and possess it for ever and ever. They actually rule along with Christ.

In His Revelation to John, Jesus said, *"To the one who is victorious, I will give the right to sit with me on my throne, just as I was victorious and sat down with my Father on his throne"* (Revelation 3:21). In his vision, John further saw: *His servants will serve him. They will see his face, and his name will be on their foreheads. And they will reign for ever and ever* (22:3-4, 5). Jesus' holy people will reign with Him forever.

Conclusion

All those who have repented of their sins, have accepted Jesus Christ as their savior, and have been living the new life with the help of the Holy Spirit have already become citizens of the kingdom of God. If they continue to live a life of victory over sin, one day they will reign with Jesus in his glorious kingdom—one that

---

[118] Set apart; saved.

will never come to an end. They will be princes and princesses in the kingdom of God.

Have you become a citizen of God's kingdom? If so, are you doing everything you can to advance the kingdom? If so, stay strong in the Real Faith. Jesus said, *"I am coming soon. Hold on to what you have, so that no one will take your crown"* (Revelation 3:11).

CHAPTER 9

Look! He Comes

As you have read so far, Jesus was a unique person in human history. Here is a list of His one-of-a-kind qualities:

- He was God who came to us as a man (Chapter 2).
- He gave His life on the cross for everyone's sins. Anyone who accepts Him will have their sins forgiven (Chapter 3).
- He died and was buried, but He rose again and left behind an empty tomb (Chapter 4).
- He ascended to Heaven, where He sits at the right hand of the Father as our High Priest (Chapter 4).
- He promised that He was always going to be with his followers, even to the end of the age (Chapter 6).
- After He returned to Heaven, He sent the Holy Spirit to be a helper to those who believe in Him (Chapter 7).
- After receiving a glorious kingdom from God the Father, He will rule forever, along with all of His followers (Chapter 8).

He also made a unique promise that no one else has ever made. He said, *"I will come back and take you to be with me that you also may be where I am"* (John 14:3). Jesus said three things in this one short sentence: (1) He will come back to this Earth, (2) He will take his followers to be with Him, and (3) His followers will be with Him where He is.

Jesus will come back a second time. He made that promise, and He **WILL** fulfill it.

Blueprint of Salvation

The Almighty God created a blueprint for the salvation of humans. The crucifixion, the resurrection, the ascension, and the return of Jesus are the four pillars of that blueprint. The Real Faith is firmly established on these four pillars. The return of Jesus is just as critical for salvation as the other three pillars of faith.

> The apostle wrote: *Christ was sacrificed once to take away the sins of many; and he will appear a second time, not to bear sin, but to bring salvation to those who are waiting for him* (Hebrews 9:28).

Today, we have the assurance of salvation. Jesus will deliver this salvation when He returns, by giving us the privilege of living with Him where He is. We have the assurance of salvation when we have an unshakable faith in all the four pillars of the blueprint. There is no other blueprint of salvation available anywhere else in the world.

The Blessed and the Cursed

In the previous chapter, you learned what Jesus said about His coming kingdom:

> "When the Son of Man comes in his glory, and all the angels with him, he will sit on his glorious throne. All the nations will be gathered before him ... . Then the King will say to those on his right, 'Come, you who are blessed by

Chapter 9

my Father; take your inheritance, the kingdom prepared for you since the creation of the world'" (Matthew 25:31-32, 34).

Six main points must be noted in this passage of Scripture about the coming of Jesus:

1. When Jesus comes back the second time, He will come in His glory—not as the humble man who came to die for the sins of humanity. Not again! This time He will come as KING OF KINGS AND LORD OF LORDS (Revelation 19:16).

2. He will come with all the angels of Heaven. John, the beloved disciple, wrote about his vision: *Then I looked and heard the voice of many angels, numbering thousands upon thousands, and ten thousand times ten thousand* (Revelation 5:11). It means that no one can actually count the number of angels. The billions of angels will accompany Jesus when He comes back.

3. He will sit on His glorious throne. In his vision, John saw the throne of God in Heaven: *"At once I was in the Spirit, and there before me was a throne in heaven with someone sitting on it. And the one who sat there had the appearance of jasper and ruby. A rainbow that shone like an emerald encircled the throne"* (Revelation 4:2-3).

4. People of all the nations will gather before Him. All will kneel before Him and acknowledge Him as Lord. Writing about Jesus, the apostles Paul and Timothy said: *God exalted him to the highest place and gave him the name that is above every name, that at the name of Jesus every knee should bow... and every tongue acknowledge that Jesus Christ is Lord, to the glory of God the Father* (Philippians 2:9–11).

5. He will separate all those who are gathered before him into two groups.

6. He will invite those on His right hand to take their place in the kingdom prepared for them. These are the believers—the blessed of God—who not only kept their faith in Jesus, but also participated in acts of mercy—feeding the hungry, housing and clothing the needy, helping the sick, and visiting the prisoners (as recorded in Matthew 25:35-36). Jesus said, *"Truly I tell you, whatever you did for one of the least of these brothers and sisters of mine, you did for me"* (Matthew 25:40). People of the Real Faith must help the needy, without expecting anything in return. Not everyone can directly engage in helping the poor and needy people, but we should support the various organizations that are involved in doing this kind of work.

You may wonder what will happen to those separated on the left. In the words of Jesus, the King will say to those on his left, *"Depart from me, you who are cursed, into the eternal fire prepared for the devil and his angels"* (25:41). Jesus then concluded His remarks by saying, *"Then they will go away to eternal punishment, but the righteous to eternal life"* (25:46).

When Jesus came the first time, He said, *"I did not come to judge the world, but to save the world"* (John 12:47). The second time when He comes in all His glory, He will come to judge the world.

The Judgment

The apostle Paul wrote: *We must all appear before the judgment seat of Christ* (2 Corinthians 5:10). The psalmist employed beautiful poetry to prophesy about the coming of the Lord to judge the Earth:

> *Worship the LORD in the splendor of his holiness;*
> *tremble before him, all the earth.*
>
> *Say among the nations, "The LORD reigns."*
> *The world is firmly established, it cannot be moved;*

Chapter 9

he will judge the peoples with equity[119].

*Let all creation rejoice before the LORD, for he comes,
he comes to judge the earth.*

*He will judge the world in righteousness
and the peoples in his faithfulness* (Psalms 96:9-10, 13).

People sometimes wonder what will happen to all those who did not even hear the name of Jesus so they could have a chance to believe in Him. The thinking is that if they perhaps had an excuse, we can have an excuse too. It is a natural human tendency to compare ourselves with others.

Suffice to say that God will judge everyone with complete fairness, and according to His holiness and faithfulness, as we have read in the above Psalm. You who have heard the Gospel must respond to the Gospel.

If you are wondering about others, here is what Jesus would say: After His resurrection, Jesus was having a conversation with His disciples. He prophesied that Peter would be crucified. Peter then turned to the beloved disciple, John, and asked Jesus, *"Lord, what about him?"* (John 21:21). Jesus answered, *"If I want him to remain alive until I return, what is that to you? You must follow me"* (21:22). We must follow Jesus, spread the Gospel message to others, and not be concerned about how He will judge the world.

Look! He Comes

John wrote, *"Look, he is coming with the clouds, and every eye will see him ..."* (Revelation 1:7). The return of Jesus will be impossible to miss, because it will be the most glorious event this world would have ever seen. *At that time they will see the Son of Man coming in a cloud with power and great glory* (Luke 21:27). Jesus will be sitting on His glorious throne, surrounded by all the holy angels of Heaven. It seems that all the inhabitants of Heaven will accompany the King of Kings and Lord of Lords. Jesus said,

---

[119] Fairness.

"*As lightning that comes from the east is visible even in the west, so will be the coming of the Son of Man*" (Matthew 24:27). The apostles Paul, Silas, and Timothy wrote that the Lord Jesus will be *revealed from heaven in blazing fire with his powerful angels* (2 Thessalonians 1:7). The entire sky will be ablaze with the glory of Jesus and His angels.

Jesus had refused to call even a single one of these powerful angels at the time of His crucifixion, so He could lay the foundation for our salvation. Without the crucifixion, neither the resurrection, nor the ascension, nor the second coming would have happened because they would have been of no use. The blueprint begins with the crucifixion of our Lord. Therefore, salvation also begins at the cross of Jesus. How thankful we ought to be that Jesus was willing to go to the cross.

The Mourners

Today, we put our faith in Jesus whom we know as the One who was *gentle and humble in heart* (Matthew 11:29); *despised and rejected by mankind, a man of suffering, and familiar with pain* (Isaiah 53:3); and the One who *was oppressed and afflicted, yet he did not open his mouth* (53:7). There were many who mocked and mistreated Jesus at His crucifixion. It is sad indeed that even today many continue to mock Him and mistreat His followers. What will they do with their mockery when they see the King of Kings coming with such dazzling glory that their eyes will be blinded?

John, the beloved disciple, wrote:

> "*Look, he is coming with the clouds,*"
> and "*every eye will see him,*
> *even those who pierced him*";
> *and all the peoples on earth* "*will mourn because of him.*"
> *So shall it be! Amen* (Revelation 1:7).

The mourners are scattered in every corner of the world. They are those who have rejected God's mercy and grace to

Chapter 9

receive salvation. They mourn because it is too late for them. Jesus is coming to judge, not to offer salvation.

How will they know that it is Jesus coming in the sky? This is what Jesus said:

> "Then will appear the sign of the Son of Man in heaven. And then all the peoples of the earth will mourn when they see the Son of Man coming on the clouds of heaven, with power and great glory" (Matthew 24:30).

Just before Jesus' return, His sign will appear in the sky for everyone to see. What is that sign? Of course, it is the cross. The only sign of Jesus that is recognized by people all over the world is the cross. When a giant sign of the cross is seen clearly across the sky, everyone will know that it is Jesus who is coming in power and great glory.

People will mourn because they had mocked and rejected this King of Kings, and there will be no more offer of salvation. But, Alas! The number of mourners will far exceed those who rejoice at His coming. That's why the phrase, *all the peoples of the earth* (24:30), is used.

> In his vision, John saw and recorded: *Then the kings of the earth, the princes, the generals, the rich, the mighty, and everyone else, both slave and free, hid in caves and among the rocks of the mountains. They called to the mountains and the rocks, "Fall on us and hide us from the face of him who sits on the throne and from the wrath of the Lamb!"* (Revelation 6:15-16).

The mockers include people from all walks of life. They are unable to bear the coming of the King of Kings. They are terrified, and they wish that they would die before they would have to face the King of Kings whom they have mocked and rejected.

The Joyful Ones

A second group of people—the believers and humble followers of Jesus—shout with joy, "*Surely this is our God; we trusted in him, and* he saved us. This is the LORD, we trusted in him; let us rejoice and be glad in his salvation" (Isaiah 25:9).

John described another scene from his vision:

> After this I looked, and there before me was a great multitude that no one could count, from every nation, tribe, people and language, standing before the throne and before the Lamb. They were wearing white robes and were holding palm branches in their hands. And they cried out in a loud voice:
>
> "Salvation belongs to our God,
> who sits on the throne,
> and to the Lamb" (Revelation 7:9-10).

An Eternal Marvel

The apostles wrote that on that day, Jesus will come *to be glorified in his holy people and to be marveled at among all those who have believed* (2 Thessalonians 1:10). Jesus will be glorified because there will be many, from all over the world, who will be welcomed into His kingdom, just as John saw in his vision.

The believers will have every reason to rejoice and praise God. The believers will marvel how the all-powerful Ruler of the Universe could come as a gentle and humble savior, why He did not open His mouth before those who mocked Him, and how He could take our place on the cross so that we could live with Him forever. We will marvel that Jesus received us while we were yet sinners. We will also marvel how a simple act of faith in Christ brought us such a huge reward for all eternity—a reward that we were not worthy of, but we received it because of the great love God had for us.

The apostle Paul wrote: *What no eye has seen, what no ear has heard, and what no human mind has conceived—the things God has prepared for those who love him* (1 Corinthians 2:9). We cannot even imagine what the real kingdom of God will be like—we will keep on marveling at the glory of God. David wrote:

Chapter 9

I will praise you, Lord my God, with all my heart;
I will glorify your name forever (Psalms 86:12).

Resurrection of Believers

While talking to His disciples about His coming, Jesus stated, *"At that time people will see the Son of Man coming in clouds with great power and glory. And he will send his angels and gather his elect from the four winds, from the ends of the earth to the ends of the heavens"* (Mark 13:26-27). The elect are those who have believed in Jesus and obeyed Him.

> The apostles wrote: *According to the Lord's word, we tell you that we who are still alive, who are left until the coming of the Lord, will certainly not precede those who have fallen asleep[120]. For the Lord himself will come down from heaven, with a loud command, with the voice of the archangel and with the trumpet call of God, and the dead in Christ will rise first. After that, we who are still alive and are left will be caught up together with them in the clouds to meet the Lord in the air. And so we will be with the Lord forever* (1 Thessalonians 4:15–17).

The apostles penned these words to encourage and give hope to those who die in Christ before He comes. Those who die in Christ are believers who were born of God (see Chapter 5) and lived a new life in the Real Faith (see Chapter 6). Jesus referred to them as the elect. They died after having accepted by faith God's blueprint of salvation. The apostles inform us quite authoritatively that the believers who have died in Christ will rise from the dead to be reunited with the Lord at His coming. When Jesus comes, both the resurrected and the living saints will meet Him together— one group will not meet Him before the other. We will be caught up together in the clouds.

---

[120] Died.

The apostle Paul wrote: *We will all be changed—in a flash, in the twinkling of an eye, at the last trumpet. For the trumpet will sound, the dead will be raised imperishable, and we will be changed. For the perishable must clothe itself with the imperishable, and the mortal with immortality* (1 Corinthians 15:51–53).

At the coming of Jesus, we will be given new bodies that will never die; we will be immortal. We will live forever with Jesus.

Conclusion

The Heavenly kingdom of God is established when Jesus returns to this Earth. He will return according to His promise, for one purpose: to take His followers with Him. Those who have died believing in Him will be raised to life. Both the living and the resurrected saints will be changed, so they will never die again. *And so we will be with the Lord forever* (1 Thessalonians 4:17).

This should be the main goal of life for every person. True, life must continue until Jesus returns. We must plan and prepare for our careers, earn a living, take care of our families, etc., but preparing for eternal life must be a critical part of how we plan our lives.

Now is the time to make the decision. Are you going to be among the great multitude wearing white robes, shouting the Lord's praises when He returns? Or, will you be among the mourners?

Are you sure? You can be sure by turning your life over to Christ if you have not already done so.

CHAPTER 10

The Enemy

The book of Revelation describes a cosmic battle. Surprisingly, this major battle between two powerful armies occurred not on the Earth, but in Heaven. John, who saw this vision, wrote:

> Then war broke out in heaven. Michael and his angels fought against the dragon, and the dragon and his angels fought back. But he was not strong enough, and they lost their place in heaven. The great dragon was hurled down—that ancient serpent called the devil, or Satan, who leads the whole world astray. He was hurled to the earth, and his angels with him (Revelation 12:7–9).

The devil, also called Satan, is given a symbolic name, "the great dragon." The book of Revelation describes a lot of scenes in symbolic imagery. So, we can't say that this is an account of an actual battle in which weaponry was used. We can conclude, however, that Heavenly beings were involved on the two opposing sides of an issue, and God was in the center of it. Of course, God won the battle, and the losing party was expelled from Heaven. They were thrown down to this Earth. John then commented:

> "Therefore rejoice, you heavens
> And you who dwell in them!
> But woe to the earth and the sea,
> because the devil has gone down to you!
> He is filled with fury[121],
> because he knows that his time is short" (12:12).

When this battle took place, Jesus was in Heaven, before He came into this world. In a discussion with His disciples, He stated, *"I saw Satan fall like lightning from heaven"* (Luke 10:18).

When we read the account from Revelation, some questions arise: What caused this war? Where did the devil come from? Did God create a devil? What is the devil doing on this Earth? What does it mean that his time is short? This chapter will answer these questions.

How Evil Began

God did not create a devil. The prophet Ezekiel used symbolism of the king of Tyre to describe the origins of Satan and evil. According to the word of the LORD that came to him, Ezekiel wrote:

> *"You were the seal of perfection,*
> *full of wisdom and perfect in beauty.*
>
> *You were in Eden, the garden of God;*
>
> *every precious stone adorned you:*
> *carnelian, chrysolite and emerald,*
> *topaz, onyx and jasper,*
> *lapis lazuli, turquoise and beryl.*
>
> *Your settings and mountings were made of gold;*
> *on the day you were created they were prepared.*
>
> *You were anointed as a guardian cherub,*
> *for so I ordained you.*

---

[121] Fierce anger.

Chapter 10

You were on the holy mount of God;
you walked among the fiery stones.

You were blameless in your ways from the day you were created
till wickedness[122] was found in you.

Through your widespread trade you were filled with violence, and you sinned.

So I drove you in disgrace from the mount of God,
and I expelled you, guardian cherub,
from among the fiery stones.

Your heart became proud on account of your beauty, and you corrupted your wisdom because of your splendor. So I threw you to the earth ..." (Ezekiel 28:12–17).

Notice a couple of similarities between this poetic account and the war account in Revelation. This being was on the mount of God (Heaven), but he was thrown down to the Earth. He was filled with violence. Here are some facts we can glean from Ezekiel's account:

1. This being was created perfect. He was the *seal of perfection, full of wisdom and perfect in beauty* (28:12). He was also highly decorated by God.

2. He was a cherub[123]. The psalmist tells us: *The LORD reigns, let the nations tremble; he sits enthroned between the cherubim*[124] (Psalms 99:1). Hence, this was one of the cherubim that served at the throne of God.

3. This cherub was blameless (sinless) from the time he was created, but he became wicked[125] at some point. Sin began with this cherub.

---

[122] Evildoing.
[123] An angel of high rank.
[124] Plural of cherub.
[125] Sinful and evildoer.

4. He *walked among the fiery stones* (Ezekiel 28:14), referring to angels in Heaven. The writer of Hebrews informs us: *In speaking of the angels he says, "He makes his angels spirits, and his servants flames of fire"* (Hebrews 1:7). So, this cherub worked with the angels in Heaven.

5. He became filled with violence, and sinned. Ezekiel writes: *Through your widespread trade you were filled with violence* (Ezekiel 28:16). It refers to a plot in which this cherub tried to get as many angels as he could on his side. It is thought that he was able to persuade a third of the angels to follow him. This idea is found in Revelation 12:4, where it says, in symbolic language, that the dragon's *tail swept a third of the stars out of the sky and flung them to the earth*. The mention of violence gives us a clue that he started the war. He very likely also threatened the other angels with violence if they refused to follow him.

6. The main cause of his sin was pride. The prophet informs us in Ezekiel 28:17 that, because of his beauty and splendor, he became proud and corrupted his wisdom. Yes, pride corrupts the mind. His thoughts turned selfish and evil as he started to focus on himself.

In summary, we find that God did not create a devil. He created a perfect cherub who served Him at His throne in Heaven. This cherub became proud and selfish, and he spread trouble among the angels. He was able to get about a third of the angels to join him in his rebellion against God. Just as we have been given the freedom to choose between obeying or disobeying God, the angels have been given the same choice.

The prophet Isaiah gives us a glimpse into the nature of the rebellion:

> *How you have fallen from heaven,*
> *morning star, son of the dawn!*
>
> *You have been cast down to the earth,*
> *you who once laid low the nations!*

Chapter 10

> *You said in your heart,*
> *"I will ascend to the heavens;*
> *I will raise my throne above the stars of God;*
> *I will sit enthroned on the mount of assembly,*
> *on the utmost heights of Mount Zaphon.*
> *I will ascend above the tops of the clouds;*
> *I will make myself like the Most High"*
> (Isaiah 14:12–14).

In this poetic narrative, "morning star" is a translation of the proper name, Lucifer. The devil's name was Lucifer before his fall from Heaven. We already know from Ezekiel's account that he was a high-ranking angel, and that pride, selfishness, and jealousy were the cause of his rebellion against God. He wanted to become like the Most High God. In other words, he wanted to topple God's government and establish his own rule. He wanted to *sit enthroned* (14:13) in the place of God. For Lucifer to think this way, He had to be a very high-ranking cherub. To carry out his plot of rebellion against God, Lucifer started the war in Heaven.

Even today, sin is rebellion against God. It was pointed out in Chapter 6 that sin is disobedience to God's commands, which is rebellion. In some commands, God requires us to do certain things, but we say, "No, I don't want to do that." In other commands, God requires us not to do certain things, but we say, "I like doing that." This is the nature of rebellion. Lucifer's example instructs us that there is no room for rebellion in Heaven. Hence, those who rebel against God's commands will not enter His kingdom.

In the Garden of God

In Ezekiel's narrative, we read that Lucifer had been in the garden of God. This takes us to the account of creation recorded in the Holy Scriptures. This is what we read about the garden:

> *Now the LORD God had planted a garden in the east, in Eden; and there he put the man he had formed. And the LORD God commanded the man, "You are free to eat from any tree in the garden; but you must not eat from the tree of the knowledge of good and evil, for when you eat from it you will certainly die." Then the LORD God made a woman from the rib he had taken out of the man, and he brought her to the man* (Genesis 2:8, 16-17, 22).

Sometime after creating the Earth, God planted a garden at a location called Eden. He also formed the first man—Adam—and the first woman—Eve. He placed them in the garden. God commanded that they must not eat the fruit of one particular tree.

At this stage, sin had not entered into the lives of the first man and woman. So, they had to be tested to see whether they should be allowed to live forever. The statement, *"When you eat from it you will certainly die"* (2:17), suggests that they could keep on living, even forever, if they continued to obey God's command. But, they were free to choose; they were *free to eat from any tree in the garden* (2:16).

Now enters the devil into the picture! He did not come as an angel, but disguised himself as a serpent. The devil employed his first trick by twisting what God had said. *He said to the woman, "Did God really say, 'You must not eat from any tree in the garden'?"* (3:1). The serpent suggested that they could eat from all the trees in the garden; God didn't really mean that any tree was off limit.

The woman countered, *"But God did say, 'You must not eat fruit from the tree that is in the middle of the garden, and you must not touch it, or you will die'"* (3:3). The serpent's first trick did not work; Eve knew God's commandment. So, the serpent came up with another trick. *"You will not certainly die,"* the serpent said to the woman. *"For God knows that when you eat from it your eyes will be opened, and you will be like God ..."* (3:4-5). This time the serpent suggested that she could not die, she was created to live forever. Besides, who does not want to be full of wisdom and knowledge like God! The woman might have thought that she should not let this opportunity slip away—the opportunity to become like God. Note that this was also Lucifer's sin, to be *like the Most High* (Isaiah 14:14).

> *When the woman saw that the fruit of the tree was good for food and pleasing to the eye, and also desirable for gaining wisdom, she took some and ate it. She also gave some to her husband, who was with her, and he ate it. Then the eyes of both of them were opened, and they realized they were naked; so they sewed fig leaves together and made coverings for themselves* (3:6-7).

This is how sin started in this world. It started with disobedience to God's command. As soon as Adam and Eve sinned, they knew that they were naked—their eyes were opened to their sinful condition. They were ashamed. So, they tried to cover themselves with fig leaves. But, sin cannot be covered with anything people may try to do on their own.

> *Then the man and his wife heard the sound of the LORD God ... and they hid from the LORD God among the trees of the garden. But the LORD God called to the man, "Where are you?"* (3:8-9).

Sin separates us from God. It makes us hide from God by engaging in rituals, visiting "holy" places, performing good deeds, reading religious books, or simply ignoring God. But, He comes looking for us. He invites us to come to His throne where we can obtain His mercy and grace, and forgiveness of sins through Jesus Christ.

Who's Responsible?

When we sin, who's responsible? The devil, or us?

God came looking for Adam and Eve. God knew they had sinned, but He wanted them to explain their action. God is a righteous judge.

> *Then the LORD God said to the woman, "What is this you have done?" The woman said, "The serpent deceived me, and I ate"* (Genesis 3:13).

But God did not accept her excuse. She knew the commandment well. She had repeated the commandment to the serpent. The lesson here is that when we know the commandments, there is no excuse for disobedience.

God requires us to take individual responsibility for our sins. He gives us the freedom to choose. If we do not enter the kingdom of God, we cannot put the blame on anyone else. We will have to take personal responsibility for our own decisions and actions.

The Enemy

After his fall, Lucifer was no longer called the "morning star." His name became Satan. The names "Satan" and "devil" both mean "adversary" or "enemy." Speaking to the serpent, God said, *"I will put enmity between you and the woman, and between your offspring and hers"* (Genesis 3:15).

Satan is the enemy of God and humans. He is also called the "evil one," "tempter," "god of this age," "prince of this world," and "accuser." His evil angels are the demons. Jesus freed many people who were possessed by demons.

Although fallen from Heaven, Satan is still a powerful spirit being. He has with him innumerable evil angels (demons) who were brought down with him to this Earth.

You must have seen pictures of an evil-looking monster with pointed ears, horns, and a tail, carrying a pitchfork, roasting people in hellfire. Satan does not look anything close to that. We know this from the descriptions of Lucifer given by the prophets of God.

God, in His supreme wisdom, did not destroy this enemy right away, just as God does not destroy us when we sin. Adam and Eve also did not die right away.

Chapter 10

Satan, however, knows that his end will come. *"You have come to a horrible end and will be no more,"* wrote the prophet (Ezekiel 28:19). John saw in his vision that *the devil ... was thrown into the lake of burning sulfur ...* (Revelation 20:10). The eternal fire described by Jesus is *prepared for the devil and his angels* (Matthew 25:41). Lucifer refused to repent of his sin and return to God to receive His mercy and grace. Pride kept him away. His destiny has been decided. Even today, many people refuse to repent because of their pride.

Satan is not in-charge of hell. He has no power to roast anyone in hellfire. He himself will be thrown into the fires of hell. He knows that his time is coming.

The example of Lucifer should warn us that the fires of hell are also reserved for those who follow Satan's example, and refuse to come to God's throne to find His mercy and grace. He has made his decision. You must make yours. The time is short. That's why now is the time to find salvation in Jesus Christ. It doesn't matter who you are. He is still waiting for you, saying, *"Here I am! I stand at the door and knock"* (Revelation 3:20).

Under the Enemy's Control

Before His crucifixion, Jesus prayed for the disciples. In this prayer, He said, *"My prayer is not that you take them out of the world but that you protect them from the evil one. They are not of the world, even as I am not of it"* (John 17:15-16). Jesus said that His followers were not of the world. What did He mean? We find the answer in the first letter John wrote to the believers: *The whole world is under the control of the evil one* (1 John 5:19). Because the world is under the devil's control, the followers of Jesus must stay away from the evils in this world by following God's commandments and living the new life described in Chapter 6.

> *Do not love the world or anything in the world. If anyone loves the world, love for the Father is not in them. For everything in the world—the lust of the flesh, the lust of*

the eyes, and the pride of life—comes not from the Father but from the world. The world and its desires pass away, but whoever does the will of God lives forever (2:15–17).

We must keep away from the evils in this world. Sinful pleasures of this world are tempting, but they are temporary. They pass away quickly.

Living in the World

We have to live in this world. Apart from our personal and family obligations, we should help the needy, as pointed out in the previous chapter. We must also have a part in sharing the Gospel with others. That will help bring many people out of Satan's dominion into God's kingdom.

It is good to have the right type of ambition. Achieving high levels of education and preparing for a career are noble goals. The test is whether the ambition is for selfish purposes, or whether it is used to help others. Paul and Timothy, servants of Jesus Christ, wrote: *Do nothing out of selfish ambition or vain conceit*[126] (Philippians 2:3). Note that these were the very sins that led to Lucifer's fall.

Opposition to the Gospel

In today's world, many evils in society are described as good by some television programs, movies, politicians, public schools, and even some religious leaders. In Jesus' day, there was no television or movies. The religious leaders were also the politicians, and ran the school system in the synagogues. Toward the end of His ministry, Jesus scolded these religious leaders: *"Woe to you, teachers of the law and Pharisees, you hypocrites! You shut the door of the kingdom of heaven in people's faces. You yourselves do not enter, nor will you let those enter who are trying to"* (Matthew 23:13).

---

[126] Pride.

Chapter 10

It is well to take note that religion does not save. Jesus is the One who saves.

To the religious leaders, Jesus also said, *"You belong to your father, the devil, and you want to carry out your father's desires"* (John 8:44). Today, the enemy works in the same way. He works through many agencies—both religious and secular—in deceiving the world. Satan is trying his best to oppose the Gospel. In many countries, governments and many religious leaders are working under Satan's influence. Many governments have passed laws against the preaching of the Gospel; they often impose severe penalties for doing so. Persecution of the followers of Jesus is intense in these countries. The devil's anger is directed at the Gospel because it is the only true message of salvation. Yet, the Gospel message is going forth, because Jesus prophesied that it will.

A Confusing World

We are living in a confusing world. Children growing up and the young people in particular are puzzled about what is right and what is wrong. There is great confusion even about faith and religion, about what is truth and what is not. The Holy Scriptures label such a state of confusion as "Babylon[127]." It is used as a symbol for a confused world. John, the beloved disciple, saw this confused world in his vision. He saw that a powerful angel descended from Heaven, *and the earth was illuminated by his splendor. With a mighty voice he shouted:*

> *"Fallen! Fallen is Babylon the Great!"*
> *She has become a dwelling for demons*
> *and a haunt for every impure spirit ... .*
>
> *For all the nations have drunk*
> *the maddening wine of her adulteries*
> (Revelation 18:1–3).

---

[127] The name "Babylon" comes from "Babel," where God had confused people's language (Genesis 11:1–9). Hence, confusion is at least one meaning of "Babylon" in the book of Revelation.

The mighty angel is a symbol for the Gospel of Jesus Christ that illuminates the whole world. It does not mean that everyone will accept the Gospel message. Jesus said that the *gospel of the kingdom will be preached in the whole world as a testimony to all nations ...* (Matthew 24:14). The Gospel is an invitation to the world to accept the Lord Jesus Christ while there is still time. The Gospel is a testimony about Jesus and His call to repentance. Everyone is called to make an individual decision to accept or not to accept the Gospel message.

Notice that this confused world, Babylon, is the habitation of demons, under the leadership of Satan. He is described as *the god of this age who has blinded the minds of unbelievers*[128], *so that they cannot see the light of the gospel that displays the glory of Christ, who is the image of God* (2 Corinthians 4:4). But, there is another voice—a gentler voice—that says, *"Come out of her, my people,"* in Revelation 18:4:

> *Then I heard another voice from heaven say:*
>
> *"Come out of her, my people,"*
> *so that you will not share in her sins,*
> *so that you will not receive any of her plagues;*
>
> *for her sins are piled up to heaven,*
> *and God has remembered her crimes.*
>
> *She will be consumed by fire,*
> *for mighty is the Lord God who judges her*
> (Revelation 18:4-5, 8).

God is calling you today to come out of the confusion of this world, and believe the Gospel. A time is coming when this world will be judged by God. At that time, there will be two groups of people. One group will remain in Babylon, the other will enter the kingdom of God.

---

[128] Those who reject the Gospel of Jesus Christ.

Chapter 10

Jesus Overcame

Satan's first defeat took place when he was kicked out of Heaven and was thrown down to this Earth. The second time, Jesus defeated Satan when he did his best to trick Him.

Before Jesus started His work of preaching, teaching, and healing, His preparation for the ministry included a face-to-face encounter with Satan:

> *Then Jesus was led by the Spirit into the wilderness to be tempted by the devil. After fasting forty days and forty nights, he was hungry. The tempter came to him and said, "If you are the Son of God, tell these stones to become bread."*
>
> *Jesus answered, "It is written: 'Man shall not live on bread alone, but on every word that comes from the mouth of God'"*[129] *(Matthew 4:1–4).*

Jesus prepared for His unique ministry by fasting. Then the devil tested Jesus by using the phrase, "If you are the Son of God." By turning stones into bread, Jesus was tempted to prove that He was indeed the Son of God. But, Jesus did not come to seek His own glory. He did not come to do wonderful works for His own benefit. Besides, there was no need for Him to prove anything to His enemy, Satan, who actually knew who Jesus was. Jesus rebuffed the devil by using the Holy Scriptures. But, then, in the second test, the devil himself quoted from Scripture:

> *Then the devil took him to the holy city and had him stand on the highest point of the temple. "If you are the Son of God," he said, "throw yourself down. For it is written:*
>
> *"'He will command his angels concerning you, and they will lift you up in their hands, so that you will not strike your foot against a stone.'"*[130]

---

[129] Jesus cited Deuteronomy 8:3.
[130] The devil cited from Psalm 91:11–12.

> *Jesus answered him, "It is also written: 'Do not put the Lord your God to the test.'"*[131] *(4:5–7).*

God fulfills His promises in accordance with His plans and purposes. We must leave that to Him. Our duty is to obey His commands. After the devil was frustrated a second time when Jesus told him who was worthy of obedience—God or the devil—the devil tried one final trick on Jesus:

> *Again, the devil took him to a very high mountain and showed him all the kingdoms of the world and their splendor. "All this I will give you," he said, "if you will bow down and worship me."*
>
> *Jesus said to him, "Away from me, Satan! For it is written: 'Worship the Lord your God, and serve him only.'"*[132]
>
> *Then the devil left him, and angels came and attended him (4:8–11).*

In the final test, the devil put in front of Jesus all the riches, luxury, rulership, and pleasures of this world. As *the god of this age* (2 Corinthians 4:4), Satan has control over the things of this world that are used to serve one's self. If only Jesus would bow down to him, He would get it all.

Had Jesus given in to any of the devil's temptations, He would have sinned, and He would have failed to save anyone. It is His absolute purity that qualified Him to be the Savior of the world. That's the reason why salvation can be found in no one else.

The Lord refused to obey Satan's commands, and stayed firm in God's commands. He then commanded Satan to get away.

We can resist temptations in the same way Jesus did. We also read: *Submit yourselves, then, to God. Resist the devil, and he will flee from you* (James 4:7). We submit to God by obeying His commandments, as found in the Ten Commandments (see Chapter 6).

---

[131] Jesus cited from Deuteronomy 6:16.
[132] Jesus based his citation on Exodus 20:5 and Deuteronomy 6:13.

Chapter 10

We resist devil's temptations with the help of the Holy Spirit. When we resist him, the devil runs away.

Conclusion

God created Lucifer as a dazzling and powerful angel, but this angel rebelled against God. He is no longer called Lucifer, the Morning Star, but Satan, the devil. When Lucifer sinned and refused to repent and obey God, He started a war in Heaven. But he was defeated and expelled from Heaven, and thrown down to this Earth. He serves as a lesson to all those who do not repent of their sins to find salvation in Jesus Christ.

God is calling people out of the confusion of this world. But each one must make an individual choice.

CHAPTER 11

Two Destinies

In this life, every person must make a choice. There are only two ways. Each leads to a different destiny. You cannot step on both of them at the same time. You must choose one way or the other. Which of the two ways you choose will settle your eternal destiny.

Two Gates and Two Roads

In a parable, Jesus said, *"Wide is the gate and broad is the road that leads to destruction, and many enter through it. But small is the gate and narrow the road that leads to life, and only a few find it"* (Matthew 7:13-14). Here, Jesus gave simple illustrations of two opposite ways.

It is fashionable to follow others. "Everybody does it," is the popular expression used by young people. "Nobody likes to be different," is another expression. You want to "fit in." The wide gate gives easy access to the broad road, where you find a lot of people. You can easily blend in. Nobody will notice any small differences you may have with others. Most of the people are having a good time, giving little or no thought to their eternal destiny.

There is another road that is not popular. The gate is small and the road is narrow. It does not look appealing, because not many people are on it. It leads in a different direction than where most people are going. Besides, you are quite comfortable on the way you are on. You don't see a need for change. But, Jesus commands, *"Enter through the narrow gate"* (7:13), because the broad road—the road you may be on—leads to destruction. Jesus has opened the narrow gate for anyone who wants to walk through it. Jesus said, *"I am the gate; whoever enters through me will be saved"* (John 10:9). That's a commitment that Jesus makes to you.

Have you entered through the narrow gate? Are you on the narrow road that leads to eternal life?

Put your trust in Jesus for the forgiveness of sins, salvation, and living the new life. The road is narrow—it is the way of the new life described in Chapter 6—but it leads to eternal life.

The narrow road is not easy. The enemy, described in the previous chapter, hates all those who walk on the narrow road. *He is filled with fury* (Revelation 12:12) toward those who walk on the road Jesus has pointed to. If you are on the narrow road, the enemy wants you to turn back and take the broad and popular road again.

Using symbolic language, the apostle Paul refers to *the flaming arrows of the evil one* (Ephesians 6:16). But, *God is faithful; he will not let you be tempted beyond what you can bear. But when you are tempted, he will also provide a way out so that you can endure it* (1 Corinthians 10:13).

Jesus knew that there would be troubles and temptations for His followers. That's why He made a precious promise: *"Peace I leave with you; my peace I give you. ... Do not let your hearts be troubled and do not be afraid"* (John 14:27). Even though the narrow road is not an easy one, Jesus walks on this road with you. His followers find peace and joy in the midst of all the problems in this world.

Chapter 11

Two Foundations

On one occasion, toward the end of a teaching session, Jesus told a parable before a large crowd. This is what He said:

> *"Therefore everyone who hears these words of mine and puts them into practice is like a wise man who built his house on the rock. The rain came down, the streams rose, and the winds blew and beat against that house; yet it did not fall, because it had its foundation on the rock"* (Matthew 7:24).

In a sense, each one of us is building a house with our lives. It includes particularly those who take the name of Jesus Christ, and call themselves Christians. You may be one of them; but, does your house have a deep foundation that is laid on the rock? The rock in this parable is the Lord Jesus Christ. Are you putting your complete trust in Him?

Then Jesus talked about a different type of foundation:

> *"But everyone who hears these words of mine and does not put them into practice is like a foolish man who built his house on sand. The rain came down, the streams rose, and the winds blew and beat against that house, and it fell with a great crash"* (7:26–27).

The shaky foundation of sand represents the things of this world—possessions, position, fame, influence, and so on—without the blessing of God. There are many Christians who have an outward form of religion, but they are not truly born again—born of God (see Chapter 5). If you happen to be one of them, you must come to Jesus and receive the gift of salvation. Unless you remain very close to Jesus, you will give up when the winds of opposition blow.

Will you be able to stand firm against hatred directed toward you as a follower of Christ? Will you stand firm in the face of persecution? Will you say "no" when an appealing temptation is presented to you? Will you follow God's commandments even when the cost of doing so is high?

A Fortress

Listen to the song of King David:

> *Yes, my soul, find rest in God;*
> *my hope comes from him.*
>
> *Truly he is my rock and my salvation;*
> *he is my fortress, I will not be shaken.*
>
> *Trust in him at all times, you people;*
> *pour out your hearts to him,*
> *for God is our refuge* (Psalms 62:5-6, 8).

Salvation comes only through Jesus Christ; by now you should have settled this issue in your mind. You can rest peacefully in God if you have found salvation in Jesus. You cannot be shaken. How so? In Jesus' name, you can pour out your heart to God in prayer when you have to face trials, persecution, and difficulties in your life.

The eyes of the Lord are on the righteous and his ears are attentive to their prayer ... (1 Peter 3:12). Whose prayers does the Lord listen to? Of those who have obtained salvation through Jesus Christ, because they are declared righteous before God. The apostles Paul and Timothy pointed out: *God made him who had no sin to be sin for us, so that in him we might become the righteousness of God* (2 Corinthians 5:21). The Sinless One who became sin for us and shed His blood on the cross on our behalf was none other than Jesus. When we accept by faith Jesus' sacrifice on the cross, God sees us as being righteous. Not because of any good thing we have done, but because of what Jesus, the Sinless One, has done. The apostle Paul stated: *This righteousness is given through faith in Jesus Christ to all who believe* (Romans 3:22).

Chapter 11

Two Kingdoms

Ever since Adam and Eve sinned in the Garden of Eden, Satan took over the rulership of this Earth. That's why he is called "the god of this age" and "the prince of this world." God is the supreme ruler of the entire vast universe, but He has permitted Satan to have rulership over this Earth. Satan will receive his final punishment in the fires of hell. Before that, however, the entire universe must see the evil results of Satan's rulership. Jesus said, *"The prince of this world now stands condemned"* (John 16:11). Satan has been judged, and he stands condemned. But, until the end of this age, Satan will continue to rule his kingdom of darkness.

You may wonder if Satan has been judged and condemned, why his kingdom of darkness has been allowed to continue. It is not for Satan's benefit. It is for your benefit and for the benefit of many who still need to find salvation in Jesus Christ. Notice what the apostle Peter wrote:

> *The Lord is not slow in keeping his promise, as some understand slowness. Instead he is patient with you, not wanting anyone to perish, but everyone to come to repentance* (2 Peter 3:9).

Today, God is waiting ever so patiently for people to receive salvation. But, one day the door of mercy will close.

Noah was a prophet of God who was sent to warn the people of his generation at the time of the great flood. Noah preached the message of God's mercy for 120 years. *Then the LORD said, "My Spirit will not contend with humans forever...* (Genesis 6:3).

> Jesus taught, *"As it was in the days of Noah, so it will be at the coming of the Son of Man. For in the days before the flood, people were eating and drinking, marrying and giving in marriage, up to the day Noah entered the ark*[133]*; and they knew nothing about what would happen until the flood came and took them all away"* (Matthew 24:37–39).

---

[133] The huge ship Noah was commanded to build.

Just like today, people were living their lives as usual. God had offered His mercy and salvation, but only Noah and his family accepted it. Similarly, people today are occupied with the things of this world. Little or no thought is being given to one's salvation. One day it will be too late.

The good news is that for those of us who have accepted Jesus, and have become His followers, God *has rescued us from the dominion of darkness and brought us into the kingdom of the Son he loves* (Colossians 1:13). To the followers of Jesus, the apostles wrote: *You are all children of the light and children of the day. We do not belong to the night or to the darkness* (1 Thessalonians 5:5).

The kingdom of darkness and the kingdom of light are two opposites. The apostles Paul and Timothy wrote:

> *The god of this age has blinded the minds of unbelievers, so that they cannot see the light of the gospel that displays the glory of Christ, who is the image of God* (2 Corinthians 4:4).

The Gospel is filled with the light of the glory of Jesus because He is the image of God the Father. But, Satan has blinded people's minds to the Gospel.

Jesus is the only One who can call people *out of darkness into his wonderful light* (1 Peter 2:9). Jesus said, "*I am the light of the world. Whoever follows me will never walk in darkness, but will have the light of life*" (John 8:12). Jesus also said to His followers, "*Take heart! I have overcome the world*" (16:33). In particular, it is Satan and his kingdom of darkness that Jesus has overcome. Hence, the apostle Paul could boldly write:

> *We are more than conquerors through him who loved us. For I am convinced that neither death nor life, neither angels nor demons, neither the present nor the future, nor any powers, neither height nor depth, nor anything else in all creation, will be able to separate us from the love of God that is in Christ Jesus our Lord* (Romans 8:37–39).

There is absolutely nothing in the entire universe that can separate us from the love of God if we continue to remain with the Lord Jesus Christ.

The kingdom of darkness is temporary. It will end when the present era comes to an end. At that time, the physical Heavenly kingdom of God—the kingdom of light—will be established, and that kingdom will be permanent. It will never end.

Two Groups

Both Jesus and John, the son of Zechariah (also known as John the Baptist), used parables to teach what would happen at the end of the age. The present era will close when Jesus comes back again. At that time, the followers of Christ will enter the physical kingdom of God. The parables given here teach us that only those who have entered through the small gate, walked on the narrow road, and built their lives on the foundation of the rock will enter the kingdom of God.

Talking about Jesus, John the Baptist informed his listeners:

> *"His winnowing fork is in his hand to clear his threshing floor and to gather the wheat into his barn, but he will burn up the chaff with unquenchable fire"* (Luke 3:17).

In many parts of the world, farmers still cut the grain using a hand sickle when it has ripened. They bring it on to a threshing floor where a farm animal treads on it to get the grain kernels out of the husk. The mixture of grain and husk is then shaken while standing up, using a fork or a flat basket. The grain falls in a pile close to the person who is winnowing. The husk (chaff) is carried by the light wind or air blowing from a fan, and falls in a different pile. In this parable, the children of light are represented by wheat and the children of darkness by chaff. Everyone will be in one group or the other. Like the wheat in the parable, only the children of light will be gathered into the kingdom of God.

In one of His parables, Jesus said:

> *"That is how it will be at the coming of the Son of Man. Two men will be in the field; one will be taken and the other left. Two women will be grinding with a hand mill; one will be taken and the other left. Therefore keep watch, because you do not know on what day your Lord will come"* (Matthew 24:39–42).

After the grain has been gathered into the barn, generally two women sit opposite each other at a round hand mill on the floor. The mill has two round millstones, one on top of the other. Holding a handle, each woman in turn rotates the top millstone as the grain is poured through an opening at the center of the millstone. That is how the grain kernels turn into flour that is used for making bread and other things. This parable also teaches that not everyone will enter the kingdom of God. Notice also that Jesus specifically used two small parables. One had two men in a field; the other had two women at the hand mill. Jesus illustrated that both men and women have an equal opportunity to enter His kingdom.

Two Choices

Today, the opportunity is open to everyone, but each person must make his/her own decision. The prophets of God always laid out two choices before the people they were sent to serve. For example, Joshua boldly proclaimed:

> *"Now fear the LORD and serve him with all faithfulness. Throw away the gods your ancestors worshiped ... and serve the LORD. But if serving the LORD seems undesirable to you, then choose for yourselves this day whom you will serve ... . But as for me and my household, we will serve the LORD"* (Joshua 24:14-15).

Moses, God's servant, said, *"I have set before you life and death, blessings and curses. Now choose life ..."* (Deuteronomy 30:19). Notice here that the true prophets of God do not use pressure, bullying, or violence. This shows what God's character is like. He simply lays before you the two choices, but you must decide. Have you made a choice about your destiny?

Conclusion

At this stage in this book, you have learned everything you need to know about God's blueprint for your salvation. The final five chapters have been written to help you strengthen your faith. Blessed are you if you have taken the first step of walking through the narrow gate. Now, keep walking on the narrow road with the Holy Spirit as your helper.

CHAPTER 12

By Faith

The Real Faith begins like a tiny seed of faith in a person's heart. The seed must first be planted so it can sprout and become a plant. Similarly, the person must believe the message of salvation, accept Jesus Christ, and obtain the gift of the Holy Spirit. The tiny plant can grow and bear fruit only when the new life is lived, as outlined in Chapter 6. A person's faith in God continues to develop as this person lives the new life. Living by faith becomes a lifelong journey.

Jesus used many parables based on seeds. Three of these parables were included in Chapter 8—The Kingdom. God's kingdom is made up of individuals who have followed God's blueprint of salvation. These are the people who have acquired the Real Faith. But, the life of faith must continue. How a person grows in faith is the subject of this chapter.

A Unique Faith

People commonly refer to various religions as faiths. In one sense, everyone in the world holds on to some type of faith— most people believe in some type of a god. Some people believe in several gods. Even those who do not believe in a god actually have faith—

they believe that there is no god. Hence, belief in something or someone is the basis of faith.

The Real Faith is also based on something and someone, but it is unique—different from all other faiths. It is different in two major ways. (1) The something that the Real Faith is based on can be put to test. It is based on the Holy Scriptures that pass the test of trustworthiness. They have proven to be credible and authentic. This is discussed in the next chapter. (2) The Real Faith is based on a unique historical figure—Jesus Christ.

As has been pointed out in previous chapters, no other person in history has been like Jesus. His one-of-a-kind qualities are summarized at the beginning of Chapter 9. He came in a unique manner; He had a unique ministry of service to people; He came for a unique purpose, to give His life for the sins of the world; He fulfilled that purpose; He rose from the dead and returned to Heaven in bodily form; and He promised to come back a second time, again in bodily form, for the whole world to see, as described in Chapter 9. At that time, He will establish His Heavenly kingdom.

Jesus' uniqueness is also attested to in a remarkable way by many prophecies that were fulfilled when He came to this Earth. Some of these prophecies have been cited in previous chapters. Here are a few that Jesus Himself could not have helped fulfill:

Birth

Jesus was born in a small town called Bethlehem:

> *"But you, Bethlehem Ephrathah, though you are small among the clans of Judah, out of you will come for me one who will be ruler over Israel, whose origins are from of old, from ancient times"* (Micah 5:2).

This prophecy was given about 700 years before the birth of Jesus. When Jesus was born, Magi[134] from the east traveled to

---

[134] Often referred to as the "wise men."

Jerusalem, and asked Herod, the king of Judea, *"Where is the one who has been born king of the Jews?"* (Matthew 2:2). Herod was disturbed by the news, because he was the king. The Jews were of the opinion that the king of the Jews—the Messiah—would establish himself as the king at his coming. So, Herod called the chief priests and teachers of the law and asked where the Messiah was to be born. They replied by citing Micah 5:2 that he would be born in Bethlehem. The Magi then traveled to Bethlehem, and found the child Jesus there with His parents.

After the Magi had left, Herod became very mad because the Magi did not go back to inform him where they had found Jesus. Murder was on Herod's mind. *He was furious, and he gave orders to kill all the boys in Bethlehem and its vicinity who were two years old and under ...* (Matthew 2:16). Before this cruel bloodshed took place, an angel of the Lord had appeared to Joseph[135] in a dream. "Get up," he said, "take the child and his mother and escape to Egypt (2:13). *After Herod died, an angel of the Lord appeared in a dream to Joseph in Egypt and said, "Get up, take the child and his mother and go to the land of Israel, for those who were trying to take the child's life are dead"* (2:19-20). This fulfilled a prophecy given by the prophet Hosea over 700 years before the birth of Jesus: *And out of Egypt I called my son* (Hosea 11:1).

Arrest

Jesus was arrested in Gethsemane, betrayed by one of his own disciples, Judas Iscariot. Jesus and His disciples paid their expenses out of donations that Judas was put in charge of. Judas was greedy. *He was a thief; as keeper of the money bag, he used to help himself to what was put into it* (John 12:6).

It had become quite well known that the chief priests were looking for a way to have Jesus killed. So, *Judas Iscariot ... went to the chief priests to betray Jesus to them. They were delighted to hear this and promised to give him money* (Mark 14:10-11). He was

---

[135] Jesus' stepfather.

paid 30 silver coins for getting the job done. This is what happened next:

> *When Judas ... saw that Jesus was condemned, he was seized with remorse and returned the thirty pieces of silver to the chief priests and the elders. "I have sinned," he said, "for I have betrayed innocent blood."*
>
> *"What is that to us?" they replied. "That's your responsibility."*
>
> *So Judas threw the money into the temple and left. Then he went away and hanged himself.*
>
> *The chief priests picked up the coins and said, "It is against the law to put this into the treasury, since it is blood money." So they decided to use the money to buy the potter's field as a burial place for foreigners* (Matthew 27:3–7).

This account is an exact fulfillment of the prophecy given by the prophet Zechariah more than 500 years before the events happened: *So they paid me thirty pieces of silver. And the LORD said to me, "Throw it to the potter" ... ! So I took the thirty pieces of silver and threw them to the potter at the house of the LORD* (Zechariah 11:12-13). Just as stated in the prophecy, Judas threw the money in the temple, and it was used to buy the potter's field, in which foreigners were buried.

Death

> *When the soldiers crucified Jesus, they took his clothes, dividing them into four shares, one for each of them, with the undergarment remaining. This garment was seamless, woven in one piece from top to bottom. "Let's not tear it," they said to one another. "Let's decide by lot who will get it"* (John 19:23-24).

This fulfilled the prophecy that King David gave almost 1,000 years before it happened: *They divide my clothes among them and cast lots for my garment* (Psalms 22:18).

Burial and Resurrection

In addition to a number of prophecies that were fulfilled at the crucifixion of Jesus, King David had also prophesied His burial and resurrection. David wrote:

Therefore my heart is glad and my tongue rejoices;
my body also will rest secure,

because you will not abandon me to the realm of the dead,
nor will you let your faithful one see decay (Psalms 16:9-10).

Jesus' body was kept secure in the grave, but it was not left there. Jesus rose from the dead on the third day before His body could begin to decay. David did not rise from the dead; so, the prophecy could not apply to him.

Based on Evidence

Faith in Jesus and the Holy Scriptures is not blind faith. It is based on evidence. Fulfillment of prophecy is evidence that the Holy Scriptures are trustworthy. Both eyewitness accounts and the fulfillment of prophecy confirm that Jesus is the Messiah, the Son of God. We have far more evidence available about Jesus than for any other person in whom people put their faith.

Yet, tragically, not everyone will believe in Him. In Jesus' day, *even after Jesus had performed so many signs in their presence, they still would not believe in him* (John 12:37). Such is the pitiful state of those who close their minds in spite of the evidence of ancient prophecies that were fulfilled in the life of Jesus.

Just like the ministry of Jesus and that of the apostles did not convince many, the Gospel will not be believed by most people. Yet, it will go out to the ends of the Earth *as a testimony to all nations, and then the end will come* (Matthew 24:14). In the end, people will be found without excuse for not accepting the salvation offered to them.

By Faith

The author of Hebrews wrote an entire chapter (Hebrews 11) on faith. This section includes a few examples from that chapter to explain what faith is.

Obedience

Obedience to God comes by faith. *By faith Abraham[136], when called to go to a place he would later receive as his inheritance, obeyed and went, even though he did not know where he was going* (Hebrews 11:8). Abraham and his father's family had settled at a place called Harran. After his father died, The LORD said to Abraham, *"Go from your country, your people and your father's household to the land I will show you. So Abram[137] went, as the LORD had told him. Abram believed the LORD, and he credited it to him as righteousness* (Genesis 12:1, 4; 15:6). Abraham was declared righteous because he took God at His word. Because he believed God, he obeyed Him.

Confidence

The author of Hebrews wrote: *Now faith is confidence in what we hope for and assurance about what we do not see. This is what the ancients were commended for* (Hebrews 11:1-2). All through the ages, faith has involved taking God at His word about things that were not obvious to the human mind. People of faith believed in God's commands. They believed in God's promises, and found assurances in those promises. They put their full confidence and hope in God, and they did whatever God had said.

---

[136] Abraham lived approximately 4,000 years ago.
[137] His name was later changed from Abram to Abraham (see Genesis 17:5).

Noah had full confidence that a great flood would come, just as God had said it would come. *By faith Noah, when warned about things not yet seen, in holy fear built an ark to save his family* (11:7).

Faith in God gives confidence, and drives out all fear of the world. *By faith Moses' parents hid him for three months after he was born, because they saw he was no ordinary child, and they were not afraid of the king's edict* (11:23). The Hebrew people were slaves in Egypt for more than 400 years. Alarmed at their growing population, the king had issued a command that required Hebrew parents to throw newborn boys into the river. Because of their faith, Moses' parents did not follow the king's orders.

The Future City

Abraham looked forward to a future city. *By faith he made his home in the promised land like a stranger in a foreign country; he lived in tents ... . For he was looking forward to the city with foundations, whose architect and builder is God* (Hebrews 11:9-10). Abraham not only believed God when told to leave Harran, but by faith he also lived as a foreigner in the country where God had brought him. But, he did not think of that country as his permanent home. By faith, Abraham looked forward to a Heavenly city.

In his vision, John saw this Heavenly city. He saw *the Holy City, Jerusalem, coming down out of heaven from God. It shone with the glory of God, and its brilliance was like that of a very precious jewel ...* (Revelation 21:10-11). This city is the New Jerusalem, prepared by God for His people who will inherit the Heavenly kingdom. To the believers in Jesus, the apostle Paul wrote:

> *What no eye has seen,*
> *what no ear has heard,*
> *and what no human mind has conceived—*
> *the things God has prepared for those who love him—*
> *these are the things God has revealed to us by his Spirit*
> (1 Corinthians 2:9-10).

The Holy Spirit bears witness to us that God has prepared unbelievably marvelous things for those who put their trust in Him.

The Faith of Abraham

The land where Abraham came to live is the piece of land where Israel and Palestine are located today. This land is occupied mainly by the Jews[138] and the Muslims[139]. Both groups hate each other. They frequently engage in violence and killings to hold on to their respective lands, and take away by force what belongs to the other group. Both claim to have the faith of Abraham.

The Real Faith of Abraham, however, is not about a piece of land on this Earth, but the city that shines with the glory of God. Just like Abraham, the followers of Jesus believe in God's promise. Jesus said:

> *"My Father's house has many rooms[140]; if that were not so, would I have told you that I am going there to prepare a place for you? And if I go and prepare a place for you, I will come back and take you to be with me that you also may be where I am"* (John 14:2-3).

Jesus says to us, "My Father's house can be your house. Come on in, if you will!" You can enter the Father's house when Jesus comes again.

The apostle Paul had the certainty of the same faith that Abraham had. To his disciple Timothy, Paul wrote:

> *I have kept the faith. Now there is in store for me the crown of righteousness, which the Lord, the righteous Judge, will award to me on that day—and not only to*

---

[138] Descendants of Abraham and those who have converted to Judaism from some other religion. They accept the Old Testament, but do not believe in Jesus as the Savior.

[139] Followers of Mohammed. He lived in Arabia (today's Saudi Arabia) between the late 6th and early 7th centuries, and proclaimed himself to be a prophet.

[140] Also translated as "dwellings" or "mansions."

Chapter 12

me, but also to all who have longed for his appearing (2 Timothy 4:7-8).

The beloved apostle of Jesus encourages all of us with his words that the crown that the Lord will give is not only for him, but also for those who believe in and long for Jesus' return. God's children will rule with Jesus in His kingdom (see the section, Rule with Him, in Chapter 8).

By faith we must look forward to that city in which Jesus has prepared mansions for us. Like Abraham, we are strangers and foreigners in this world. This is not to be our permanent home.

About the Real Faith, the apostle Paul wrote:

So in Christ Jesus you are all children of God through faith, for all of you who were baptized into Christ have clothed yourselves with Christ. There is neither Jew nor Gentile, neither slave nor free, nor is there male and female, for you are all one in Christ Jesus. If you belong to Christ, then you are Abraham's seed, and heirs according to the promise (Galatians 3:26–29).

Those who belong to Christ are Abraham's children, in a spiritual sense. Abraham actually believed and put his faith in Jesus. In Jesus' day, the Jews used to take great pride in telling others that they were Abraham's children. One day, the Jews were arguing with Jesus when He told them that He had come from God to set people free from sin. Then, they confronted Jesus by asking, *"Are you greater than our father Abraham?"* (John 8:53). In His reply, Jesus said, *"Your father Abraham rejoiced at the thought of seeing my day; he saw it and was glad"* (8:56). Abraham had faith that God would send Jesus as the savior of the world, and he was glad for it.

We can say that we have the faith of Abraham only if we have fully accepted Jesus Christ through faith. Like Abraham, the followers of Jesus from all walks of life look forward to the city that God has prepared for them. God will surely fulfill this promise one day.

Move Forward

The apostle wrote these words from God: *"But my righteous one will live by faith. And I take no pleasure in the one who shrinks back"* (Hebrews 10:38). He further wrote: *But we do not belong to those who shrink back and are destroyed, but to those who have faith and are saved* (10:39). Faith in God makes us move forward and grow spiritually. God is displeased with those who turn back. Going backward will only lead to destruction and the loss of our salvation. Salvation is for those who have faith.

About Abraham's faith, the Scriptures note:

> *He did not waver through unbelief regarding the promise of God, but was strengthened in his faith ... being fully persuaded that God had power to do what he had promised.* (Romans 4:20-21).

Today, we have firm assurances given in the Holy Scriptures. They are based on God's promises. Like Abraham, we must not waver in unbelief, but have faith that God will fulfill all of His promises.

We have assurances of salvation and of entry into God's kingdom when Jesus comes again. We cannot see it with our physical eyes. But, we can have confidence in what God has revealed through Jesus, the prophets, and the apostles. Jesus has given us the assurance that all of God's promises will be fulfilled. His death, resurrection, return to Heaven, and promise to come back are more than what we need as assurances.

Conclusion

Through faith in Christ, you can have full assurance that all your sins have been forgiven. This is a promise God has made. The Lord said through His servant, David:

Chapter 12

Blessed is the one whose transgressions are forgiven, whose sins are covered.

Blessed is the one whose sin the LORD does not count against them and in whose spirit is no deceit (Psalms 32:1-2).

The blessed ones whose sins are forgiven will one day live in the glorious city whose architect and builder is God. They will live in it forever along with Abraham and many others who have put their faith and trust in the Lord Jesus Christ.

CHAPTER 13

The Book of Books

The Holy Scriptures—commonly known as the Bible—are unique in the world. The Bible is unique in the way it was written and handed down, unlike any other book. God has made Himself known in the Holy Scriptures. Hence, the Bible is the only source for understanding who God is, what His character is like, and what He requires of us. These topics have already been covered in previous chapters. Chapters 2 and 7 explained the nature of the Deity. Chapter 3 discussed His character. Chapters 5 and 6 focused on what God requires of us.

The Bible also reveals the nature of mankind, and what the human destiny is. The Holy Scriptures help us understand why the world is in a mess. It is because of lawlessness (sin) that causes hatred, violence, and war. Yet, God sustains the natural beauty of His creation that is often awe inspiring. He also works through His followers to bring light into a dark world.

Finally, the Bible is a prophetic book. Many prophecies, given hundreds of years in advance, have already been fulfilled, as has been pointed out in previous chapters. Other remaining prophecies will be fulfilled in the future. How the evil in this world will come to an end is clearly pointed out. Above all, the Bible is full of hope for the future, for those who accept its message and live by it.

No other book in the world gives the kind of hope discussed in the previous chapters.

God's Word

Those who study the Holy Scriptures with an open and sincere mind will find that the Bible is indeed God's Word. In accordance with God's own word, the Bible has stood the test of time. God has declared:

> *"As the rain and the snow come down from heaven,*
> *and do not return to it without watering the earth ...*
>
> *so is my word that goes out from my mouth:*
> *It will not return to me empty,*
>
> *but will accomplish what I desire*
> *and achieve the purpose for which I sent it"*
> (Isaiah 55:10-11).

God's Word, contained in the Holy Scriptures, will accomplish its purpose. We can be certain of that. The prophet Isaiah also wrote:

> *"The grass withers and the flowers fall, but the word of*
> *our God endures forever"* (Isaiah 40:8).

The words given through Isaiah are prophecies as well as promises. All through history, and right up to our present time, people have tried to destroy the Holy Scriptures. Evildoers may burn the paper on which the Scriptures are printed, but they cannot silence their message. There are countries in which their rulers and governments have barred the Holy Scriptures. For example, it is illegal to take even your personal Bible with you into Saudi Arabia. They are so terrified of the Bible, because it is the Word of God that changes lives.

Chapter 13

It Marches On

Despite opposition, the Bible is available today in more languages than at any other time in history (see Footnote 87). No other book in history has ever been translated into as many languages as the Bible has been. The work of Bible translation and distribution continues on to reach as many people as possible in their native languages. Also, in accordance with God's Word, His message of grace is crossing all human barriers via radio, television, and the Internet. This will continue till the end of the present age.

There are countries today in which some religion or the other dominates the people. A relatively small number of Christ's followers are also citizens of these countries. There have been instances in which a follower of Christ may have innocently torn a piece of paper on which some text from a book considered holy by the dominant religion may have been written. In such instances, the followers of Christ have been burned alive or killed in other ways by mobs following the dominant religion. Such evil behavior does not come from God. We can be certain of that, because it is not in agreement with God's character or any command in the Holy Scriptures.

The One true God does not need human protection. He has given His Word for the salvation of mankind. The God of the Holy Scriptures is Almighty. He is perfectly capable of protecting His own Word, and to ensure that its message goes forward as a witness to all. This has been seen throughout history, despite human fury and hatred toward His Word. In the various efforts to stop God's message from going forward, we actually see Satan at work, who is *filled with fury, because he knows that his time is short* (Revelation 12:12).

The Bible has been subjected to the most intense examination, analysis, and criticism of any book in history. But, the Holy Scriptures have stood the test. At every turn, the skeptics have been silenced. But, in accordance with biblical prophecy, many still refuse to believe. Of course, God Himself has given them that choice. He declared through His servant Joshua, *"Choose for yourselves this day ..."* (Joshua 24:15).

Once Jesus and His disciples were passing through a village in which people did not welcome them. It was because they did not have the same beliefs as Jesus did.

> *When the disciples James and John saw this, they asked, "Lord, do you want us to call fire down from heaven to destroy them?" But Jesus turned and rebuked them. Then he and his disciples went to another village* (Luke 9:54–56).

Even today, Jesus speaks to people through His Word—the Bible. When some do not accept it, He moves on to other people.

The Book of Books

The Bible is often referred to as the "book of books." The word "Bible" simply means "books." It is a collection of 66 books—39 comprise what we refer to as the Old Testament, and 27 are in the New Testament. The terms "old" and "new" simply mark a division to separate the books that were written before the birth of Jesus from those written after His resurrection and ascension to Heaven. The division into the two major parts is a convenient way to refer to the various books.

The book of Psalms is the longest. It is a book of sacred hymns, or songs, written to praise God. During the time of King David, many of the Psalms were set to music. The shortest book is III John[141], a letter written by John, the beloved disciple of Jesus.

Who Wrote Them?

There are only two relatively small portions of the Holy Scriptures that God wrote. You should already know the first one—it is the Ten Commandments (see the section, God's Law, in Chapter 6).

---

[141] Actually, both II John and III John are about equal in length.

Chapter 13

The second text consists of just four words recorded in the book of Daniel: *MENE, MENE, TEKEL, PARSIN* (Daniel 5:25). These words were written supernaturally in the Aramaic language on the palace walls of King Belshazzar in Babylon. They could have been written by an angel sent from Heaven, but the words came from the throne of God. Belshazzar was openly defying God and making a mockery of Him during a banquet attended by more than a thousand invited guests. The four words pronounced judgment on the king and his kingdom. That very night Belshazzar died, and his kingdom was taken away.

The 66 books of the Bible were written by some 40 different authors over a time span of approximately 1,500 years. The oldest of the books were written somewhere around 3,500 to 4,000 years ago—very likely the most ancient records in the world. The latest book in the New Testament was written somewhere between 20 and 50 years after the ascension of Jesus Christ—now almost 2,000 years ago.

It is a wonder. The numerous authors lived in different time periods. Most did not have the opportunity to consult each other. They wrote their own books. Yet, when the books have been collected into one volume, the Bible, the messages of the 40 some authors agree. The writings differ in style, but the message remains the same. Even this short book that you are reading contains citations from half of the Old Testament books and all of the New Testament, except for four very short letters. You can see that the message is uniform in the 16 chapters of this book.

The Old Testament was written in Hebrew, along with small portions in Aramaic. The New Testament was written in Greek. The Bibles commonly read today are translations from these original languages.

The assembly of the 66 books into one Bible also took place under divine guidance. Thus, the first book called, Genesis, begins with creation and the fall of humans into sin because of disobedience. The last book, Revelation, ends with the description of a new Heaven and a new Earth in which all the men, women, and children saved by Jesus Christ live in perfect joy forever with God. The Bible became complete with this last book.

The Authors

With the two exceptions pointed out earlier, writing of the Holy Scriptures was committed to men chosen by God. That's why Jesus did not write any portion of the Holy Scriptures. The apostle Peter explained how the Scriptures were given:

> *Above all, you must understand that no prophecy of Scripture came about by the prophet's own interpretation of things. For prophecy never had its origin in the human will, but prophets, though human, spoke from God as they were carried along by the Holy Spirit* (2 Peter 1:20-21).

The Holy Spirit—the third person of the Deity, as pointed out in Chapter 7—was the agent who gave the Holy Scriptures through God's prophets. A prophet is someone who brings a message from God, and also predicts the future under Heavenly guidance. Hence, all the writers of the Holy Scriptures can be referred to as prophets. There are four main points to note in the above passage: (1) The Scriptures are written by the prophets of God. They were chosen by God to be His prophets. They all maintained a firm faith in God, even when they experienced intense opposition and persecution. (2) The Scriptures were not written according to the prophets' own interpretation of the messages they were given. They wrote the messages as given. (3) The Scriptures did not have their origin in human will. The prophets did not write what they themselves would have liked to write. (4) The prophets spoke (wrote) from God as the Holy Spirit influenced them.

The Holy Spirit used different methods to give the content of the Holy Scriptures. Sometimes a prophet was told what to write, perhaps word for word. At other times, a prophet was given visions of past, present, or future events. They were then instructed to describe in their own words what they saw and heard in the visions. In other situations, the prophet's mind was saturated by the Holy Spirit. In this case, the prophet used his own words to write the messages given to him. But, through it all, God the Holy Spirit is the real author of the Holy Scriptures. That's why the message of salvation, the rulership of God in Heaven and on Earth, the human condition and its cause, God's involvement in human affairs, and the final victory in Jesus Christ run through the Holy Scriptures like a golden thread.

Is It Complete?

The Bible, as we have it today, is the complete set of Holy Scriptures. A number of other books have been discovered. Sometimes the titles of these books give the impression that they were somehow left out of the Bible, but that is not so. There are good reasons why these books are not part of the Bible. For example, a manuscript[142] called "Letter of Jeremiah" states that the Jewish people would be captives in Babylon for seven generations. This does not agree with what the real prophet Jeremiah had prophesied:

> *The LORD Almighty says this: "Because you have not listened to my words, I will summon all the peoples of the north and my servant Nebuchadnezzar king of Babylon ... and I will bring them against this land and its inhabitants ... . This whole country will become a desolate wasteland, and these nations will serve the king of Babylon seventy years"* (Jeremiah 25:8-9, 11).

Jeremiah wrote further: *This is what the LORD says: "When seventy years are completed for Babylon, I will come to you and fulfill my good promise to bring you back to this place"* (29:10). This was an important prophecy for the people of Israel to let them know that they were not going to be captives in Babylon forever. Notice the difference in the time period covering the captivity. The fake Jeremiah wrote that it would be seven generations. The real

---

[142] A book written by hand.

prophet wrote that it would be 70 years—between one and two generations. History confirms that the captivity was for 70 years, just as the Lord had said through His true prophet.

Several false books have also been credited to some of the disciples of Jesus. Books such as the "Gospel of Thomas" have attracted readers. For one, these books were written much later than the books of the New Testament. Also, these false books contain fanciful tales for which there is no basis in the New Testament. Overall, they do not agree with the New Testament.

Some of the notable leaders of the early Christian movement were Irenaeus, Origen, and Polycarp, to name just three. Neither these nor other leaders quoted from the false books in their large amount of writings that can be read today. Irenaeus, for example, who was born roughly 100 years after the resurrection and ascension of Jesus, quoted from all books of the New Testament (except for the two smallest ones) in his writings.[143] We can have confidence that the New Testament we have today is complete.

The Purpose

This is what the apostle Paul wrote to counsel his young disciple, Timothy:

> *Evildoers and impostors[144] will go from bad to worse, deceiving and being deceived. But as for you, continue in what you have learned and have become convinced of ... and how from infancy you have known the Holy Scriptures, which are able to make you wise for salvation through faith in Christ Jesus. All Scripture is God-breathed[145] and is useful for teaching, rebuking, correcting and training in righteousness, so that the servant of God*

---

[143] Joseph M. Holden and Norman Geisler, *The Popular Handbook of Archaeology and the Bible* (Harvest House Publishers, 2013), 126.

[144] Fakes.

[145] Both the Hebrew and Greek languages use the same words for "breath" and "spirit." The Holy Scriptures are inspired by the Spirit of God, the Holy Spirit.

Chapter 13

may be thoroughly equipped for every good work (2 Timothy 3:13–17).

This short passage pretty much summarizes the purpose for which the Bible has been handed down to us. Knowing the Holy Scriptures gives protection against spiritual deceptions, because the Bible is the truth. In a prayer for His disciples, Jesus prayed, *"Sanctify them by the truth; your word is truth* (John 17:17). Above all, the Holy Scriptures point to salvation through faith in Jesus Christ. They also instruct us in how to live the new life.

Can We Understand?

Sometimes, people say that they cannot understand the Bible. There can be four main reasons for that. (1) Perhaps the most important reason is that they have not accepted the basic message of the Bible, which is forgiveness of sins through repentance by accepting Jesus Christ (see Chapter 5). This basic message can be understood by all. For example, the statement "whoever believes in Jesus Christ will not perish but will have everlasting life" is simple and clear. For further understanding of the Scriptures, a born-again person's mind is illuminated by the Holy Spirit who inspired the writers of the Holy Scriptures. (2) The Bible is sometimes misused to engage in arguments and disputes with other people. The Bible is given so we can learn the truth, and obey God. That's the kind of *training in righteousness* (2 Timothy 3:16) God desires for us to have. (3) As pointed out previously, the Holy Scriptures were written over a span of approximately 1,500 years. Many of the messages and teachings—particularly in the Old Testament, but some in the New Testament as well—were written for people living at the time the messages were given. Such messages have historical value. Yet, the Scriptures contain much that has meaning and teaching value for us today. The application of Old Testament scriptures by Jesus and His apostles, as recorded in the New Testament, is particularly useful for our learning. (4) Irregular study of the Scriptures weakens one's ability to understand them. For a better understanding, regular, prayerful study is important.

The book of Revelation, the last book of the New Testament, is highly symbolic and prophetic. The proper use of prophecy is discussed in the next chapter.

Has It Been Changed?

As stated earlier, God has been the guardian of His own Word. He has ensured that the Word we have today can be trusted. Besides, God has provided many proofs to our satisfaction if we want to believe. No proof is ever going to be adequate for those who do not want to believe.

Two major witnesses testify to the accuracy of the Old Testament we have today: (1) The Old Testament was translated from Hebrew and Aramaic into Greek somewhere between two and three hundred years before the birth of Jesus. Among scholars, this translation is known as the Septuagint. This early translation of the Bible closely matches the Old Testament we have today, well more than 2,000 years later. (2) In the late 1940s, a number of manuscripts were discovered in the desert mountainous caves located above the Dead Sea in Israel. These manuscripts were preserved in large earthen jars, and are known as the Dead Sea Scrolls[146]. Some of these manuscripts were copied more than 200 years before the birth of Jesus from older manuscripts. Among these scrolls are portions of all the books in the Old Testament, except the book of Esther. The collection includes a complete Isaiah scroll.[147] This scroll closely matches the book of Isaiah we have in our Bibles today.

Until the invention of the printing press around the year 1440, books were copied by hand. That was also the case with the Bible. Although come copying errors normally occur, the New Testa-

---

[146] Ancient books were written with ink on animal skins which were then rolled into scrolls.

[147] The Isaiah scroll and many other Dead Sea manuscripts can be seen today in the Shrine of the Book in Jerusalem, Israel.

ment has been found to be more accurately copied than any other book from ancient history.[148]

There are relatively small variations in the ancient manuscripts of both the Old and New Testaments. These variations, however, do not change the message of the Bible. For example, if a verse is unclear in one passage of Scripture, or even when a verse is missing from a certain manuscript, another passage of Scripture fills in the gap. Hence, overall, practically nothing is missing. We can read the book of books with great confidence. God had entrusted to humans the writing and copying of His Book. In spite of human weaknesses, God has watched over His Book.

People around the world have always held their own religious books in the highest regard. They dare not change their own religious books, because they fear the anger of their gods. Yet, there are those who accuse the Jewish people of changing the Old Testament, and Christians of changing the New Testament. Such attacks have proven to be baseless and absurd. The false accusations about changes made to the Holy Scriptures actually discredit the sources where such claims have originated.

Reliability

The Bible's reliability has been established mainly by means of history, archeology[149], and fulfillment of prophecy. No other literature in this world has stood the test of all three taken together.

The historical accounts recorded in the first book of the Bible, Genesis, were fully accepted as historical by Jesus and the writers of the New Testament. For example, Jesus said, *"Very truly I tell you ... before Abraham was born, I am!"* (John 8:58). By this statement, Jesus gave us the assurance that Abraham was a historical person. From the book of Genesis, Jesus also referred to the creation of this world, Adam and Eve, Noah and the great flood, and Lot.

---

[148] Joseph M. Holden and Norman Geisler, *The Popular Handbook of Archaeology and the Bible* (Harvest House Publishers, 2013), 127.

[149] Study of ancient people and events from evidence found through systematic diggings on ancient sites.

Hence, if we believe in Jesus, we also have to believe that Genesis and other Scriptures are historical.

Notice that Jesus referred to Himself as "I am," not "I was." This is the name for God that Moses was commanded to use: *God said to Moses, "... This is what you are to say to the Israelites: 'I AM has sent me to you'"* (Exodus 3:14). The name "I AM" means someone who has always existed and always will. So, Jesus, the "I AM," believed in the history recorded in the Old Testament scriptures. So did His apostles. And, so must we.

History and archeology go hand in hand. Archeology has confirmed many of the people and places recorded in the Old Testament. To give just one example, Belshazzar (mentioned earlier in this chapter) was at one time regarded as an imaginary person by critics of the Bible. Then, in 1854, a large clay cylinder[150] was discovered in the area where the city of Babylon had once existed. The name Belshazzar was found engraved in the text on this cylinder. Similarly, at least 60 names given in the Old Testament have been verified through archeology. Equally important is the fact that no archeological discovery has shown anything in the Bible to be incorrect.

As for the New Testament, the 27 books were written by eight or nine main authors. They were eyewitnesses of the events they recorded. Luke had first-hand information about Jesus and His teachings from the apostles who were eyewitnesses.[151] All of the eyewitnesses give the same basic message about Jesus. Luke, a doctor, was an accurate historian who wrote the books of Luke and Acts. In the book of Acts, we find detailed geographic, cultural, and economic descriptions of a number of places that only someone who actually had been there could have written. The apostle Paul testified that the Gospel he preached was not given to him by any man; rather, he *received it by revelation from Jesus Christ* (Galatians 1:12). Paul wrote from his personal experience with Jesus Christ.

---

[150] Archeologists have named this cylinder "the Nabonidus Cylinder."
[151] As Luke himself stated in Luke 1:1–3.

Chapter 13

There are about a dozen nonbiblical historians who have testified that Jesus was a historical person. Thallus, Josephus, Tacitus, and Pliny are some of these historians. Archeology has demonstrated that the places mentioned in the New Testament, such as the Pool of Siloam, the Pool of Bethesda, the Temple Mount, the Mount of Olives, the Synagogue of Capernaum, Nazareth, Cana, etc., are all real places that one can visit today in Israel. Archeologists have also discovered many places mentioned in the Old Testament.

The reliability of the Bible based on fulfilled prophecy is discussed in the next chapter.

The Ruler and Lamp

The Bible serves the purpose of a measuring ruler. We use a ruler to verify whether or not the stated length of something is accurate. Similarly, the Bible must be used to verify the credibility of what is written in other books and what other people teach. If other writings or teachings about the way of salvation, the new life, and human destiny do not agree with the Bible, they must be rejected.

God had entrusted the Old Testament writings to the Jews. They were made custodians of the Old Testament scriptures. The apostle Paul wrote: *The Jews have been entrusted with the very words of God* (Roman 3:2). The Jewish scribes who copied the Scriptures were very careful in making sure that the Old Testament was passed on from one generation to the next in an accurate form. As explained previously, the first Greek translation of the Old Testament and the Dead Sea Scrolls attest to the reliability of the 39 books in the Old Testament.

Regarding the New Testament, the apostle Paul made it very clear: *"Even if we or an angel from heaven should preach a gospel other than the one we preached to you, let them be under God's curse!"* (Galatians 1:8). This is strong warning, because there are many false teachings. There is no Gospel other than the one we have in the Holy Scriptures. Hence, the Bible must be used as a ruler to find out if a teaching is true.

In thanksgiving to God for His Word, the psalmist wrote: *Your word is a lamp for my feet, a light on my path* (Psalms 119:105). We can depend on the Holy Scriptures to show us the way in this life.

You are always safe following the book of books. By the same token, do not stay with a religious organization that does not uphold the Word of God, and where the teaching and preaching are mostly human words with barely a reference to the Bible. Actually, true teaching and preaching must be from the Holy Scriptures.

It has become fashionable in many organizations to dilute God's Word, because it rebukes sin. This is what the author of Hebrews wrote:

> *For the word of God is alive and active. Sharper than any double-edged sword, it penetrates even to dividing soul and spirit, joints and marrow; it judges the thoughts and attitudes of the heart* (Hebrews 4:12).

Study of the Word of God is essential, because it helps us to stay on the straight and narrow path that Jesus mentioned. It helps a believer live the life of faith.

Conclusion

The Bible is a complete and reliable book. We can be confident that we are reading the Word of God as it was given to the prophets. Regular study of the Scriptures can prevent many pitfalls in our lives. It strengthens our faith for daily living, and gives us hope for the future.

CHAPTER 14

News in Advance

The Holy Scriptures are unique because they contain many prophecies. They include prophecies that have come to pass, and many that are for the future. In a sense, prophecy is news given in advance. Although we can know what will happen in the future, we cannot know when the prophecies will be fulfilled. By having faith in prophecies that have already been fulfilled, however, we can be certain that prophecies about the future will also be fulfilled in their own time.

The Author of Prophecy

God is the author of true prophecy, because He knows everything about the future. Here is what He said through the prophet Isaiah:

> "*Remember the former things, those of long ago;*
> *I am God, and there is no other;*
> *I am God, and there is none like me.*
>
> *I make known the end from the beginning,*
> *from ancient times, what is still to come.*
> *I say, 'My purpose will stand,*
> *and I will do all that I please'*" (Isaiah 46:9-10).

God has made known to us the end from the beginning—future events before they happen. Like news in advance, God's plans and purposes—what He will do in the future—have been made known in the Holy Scriptures.

In a mocking way, God throws a challenge to all false gods that people believe in:

> *"Tell us what the former things were,*
> *so that we may consider them*
> *and know their final outcome.*
>
> *"Or declare to us the things to come,*
> *tell us what the future holds,*
> *so we may know that you are gods.*
>
> *"But you are less than nothing*
> *and your works are utterly worthless;*
> *whoever chooses you is detestable"* (41:22-23, 24).

False gods cannot explain why certain things happened in the past. False religious books either do not record much history, or they record history that contains many errors. False gods have no knowledge of what will happen in the future. Hence, not surprisingly, prophecy is missing in false religious books. If they do contain some prophecies, at least some have turned out to be incorrect.

Only the true God—who we get to know from the Bible—can explain why certain things happened in the past, and what the future holds. In the eyes of God, false gods are worthless, and whoever follows them is detestable. God challenges you to leave behind any false gods, and follow the One true God.

Prophecy serves two main purposes: (1) It gives us confidence in identifying the true God and His true Word through prophecies that have already been fulfilled. (2) It is a warning to people about things to come. The warning is often in the context of salvation, because salvation is what the Bible is mainly about. God warns us so we may pay attention to things that will happen, and arrange our lives so we are not caught off guard.

Chapter 14

The Giving of Prophecy

All true prophecy originates with God. He then transmits it to His chosen prophets.

> *Surely the Sovereign LORD does nothing without revealing his plan to his servants the prophets* (Amos 3:7).

God has revealed to His prophets His plans and purposes. Hence, in the writings of the Holy Scriptures, we have messages from God. These messages have been written for the benefit of all generations.

God reminds us that His prophetic Word has been fulfilled in the past. He declares things to come, which will also be fulfilled. He said through the prophet Isaiah:

> "*See, the former things have taken place, and new things I declare: before they spring into being I announce them to you*" (Isaiah 42.9).

God who gives prophecy also fulfills His prophetic Word. God Himself explains how He does it:

> "*I foretold the former things long ago, my mouth announced them and I made them known; then suddenly I acted, and they came to pass*" (48:3).

It is not surprising that the Lord God acts on His Word to fulfill it when the time comes. This is how prophecies are fulfilled—God acting on His Word. From the giving of prophecy to its fulfillment, we see God acting in human affairs. Hence, prophecy and history often go hand in hand.

The Rise and Fall of Empires

One of the most fascinating prophecies that has found its fulfillment in history was given by the prophet Daniel. Among other Jews, Daniel was taken captive to Babylon. He gained King Nebuchadnezzar's favor and rose to a high position in the king's administration.

The king had a dream that troubled him greatly. The wise men of Babylon could not explain to the king what his dream was and what it meant. In a vision, God revealed the dream and its meaning to Daniel, because God is the One who had given the dream to Nebuchadnezzar. So, the prophet went to the king and explained:

> "Your Majesty looked, and there before you stood a large statue—an enormous, dazzling statue, awesome in appearance. The head of the statue was made of pure gold, its chest and arms of silver, its belly and thighs of bronze, its legs of iron, its feet partly of iron and partly of baked clay. While you were watching, a rock was cut out, but not by human hands. It struck the statue on its feet of iron and clay and smashed them" (Daniel 2:31–34).

Then the prophet went on to explain the meaning of the king's dream:

> "Your Majesty... . You are that head of gold. After you, another kingdom will arise, inferior to yours. Next, a third kingdom, one of bronze, will rule over the whole earth. Finally, there will be a fourth kingdom, strong as iron ... and as iron breaks things to pieces, so it will crush and break all the others. Just as you saw that the feet and toes were partly of baked clay and partly of iron, so this will be a divided kingdom; yet it will have some of the strength of iron in it ..." (2:37, 38–41).

According to Daniel's explanation, King Nebuchadnezzar's dream foretold the rise and fall of four great empires. Babylon as a kingdom had reached its most glorious years under Nebuchadnezzar. The reassembled beautiful Ishtar Gate from ancient Babylon can be seen today in Berlin's Pergamon Museum. It bears witness to the glory of Babylon under Nebuchadnezzar, approximately 2,600 years ago. Babylon had become a powerful empire. Then, as foretold by God, this kingdom was to fall and be replaced by an inferior kingdom.

Chapter 14

The fall of Babylon occurred during Belshazzar's banquet (see the section, Who Wrote Them?, in Chapter 13). That night, Cyrus, the king of Persia, captured Babylon, in 539 B.C.[152] It was the beginning of the Persian Empire represented by the chest and hands of silver. It should be noted that, at times, God uses nonbelievers to accomplish his plans and purposes. He used Cyrus to bring the Jews back to their homeland from Babylonian captivity to rebuild Jerusalem and the temple, which were in ruins. More than 100 years before Cyrus was even born, Isaiah wrote a prophecy in which Cyrus is identified by name:

> *"I am the LORD ... who carries out the words of his servants and fulfills the predictions of his messengers ... who says of Cyrus, 'He is my shepherd and will accomplish all that I please; he will say of Jerusalem, "Let it be rebuilt," and of the temple, "Let its foundations be laid"'"* (Isaiah 44:24, 26, 28).

Next to come on the world scene, the Macedonian kingdom united the various Greek cities into one state. Alexander the Great expanded this kingdom. Then, with the ambition to spread Greek culture in the rest of the world, the 25-year old Alexander conquered the Persian Empire by defeating Darius III in at least three major battles. By 331 B.C., Alexander had conquered the Persians. At this point in history, the empire represented by silver was replaced by the one represented by bronze in Nebuchadnezzar's dream. Just four years later, Alexander had reached northwest India. While returning from India, because his troops had refused to go any further, Alexander died at the age of 32. Alexander's empire, however, continued under four of his military generals who divided the empire into four.

History shows that the fourth kingdom, represented by the legs of iron in Nebuchadnezzar's dream, was the Roman Empire. This powerful empire conquered Macedonia and the other Hellenistic (Greek) territories between 168 and 30 B.C. Represented by iron,

---

[152] Before Christ.

the cruelty of Roman emperors, who called themselves gods, is well-recorded in history.

It is absolutely stunning that the dream God gave to Nebuchadnezzar, covering world history that spanned 500 years, was given in advance. Nothing even comes close to this in any other literature. This should leave no room for doubting the Word of God. We should cry out with the apostle Peter:

> "We also have the prophetic message as something completely reliable, and you will do well to pay attention to it, as to a light shining in a dark place ..." (2 Peter 1:19).

After the Four Empires

The nations of Europe are represented by the feet of the statue that Nebuchadnezzar saw—the *feet partly of iron and partly of baked clay* (Daniel 2:33). We know from history that the Roman Empire eventually fell. Taking advantage of Rome's internal corruption and disorder, various tribes from the north were successful in sacking Rome. As the Roman Empire was crumbling, Europe was emerging into separate nations. These countries, however, were not unified nations, as they are today. Various kings and nobles ruled portions of each country. These rulers tried to hold on to territories that often changed hands between various rulers. Some of the European nations, such as France and Spain, had become unified, and they became economically powerful. The prophet Daniel had said: *This will be a divided kingdom; yet it will have some of the strength of iron in it ...* (2:41).

News about the Future

Today's Europe consists of various nation-states. The prophecy had specified: *Just as you saw the iron mixed with baked clay, so the people will be a mixture and will not remain united, any more than iron mixes with clay* (Daniel 2:43). This is very remarkable. The nations of Europe have a mixture of people through intermarriages. But, according to prophecy, the nations *will not remain united* (2:43).

Chapter 14

During the last 70 years or so, European leaders have made remarkable progress in trying to achieve economic cooperation. These efforts resulted in the formation of the European Union. The member nations of the European Union even use a common currency, the Euro. The prophecy, however, says that these nations will not remain united. That is still in the future, and we have to wait and see how it is going to unfold and when.

Nebuchadnezzar's dream continues on to the end of this age. That makes it the longest period in prophecy recorded in the Bible. We further read Daniel's words spoken to Nebuchadnezzar:

> *"While you were watching, a rock was cut out, but not by human hands. It struck the statue on its feet of iron and clay and smashed them. Then the iron, the clay, the bronze, the silver and the gold were all broken to pieces and became like chaff[153] on a threshing floor in the summer. The wind swept them away without leaving a trace. But the rock that struck the statue became a huge mountain and filled the whole earth"* (2:34-35).

Of particular note is the fact that the feet of iron mixed with clay represent the final stage of this world's history. At some point, a rock is cut supernaturally, and it smashes the entire image representing earthly political powers. This is how Daniel explained this last portion of the dream:

> *"In the time of those kings, the God of heaven will set up a kingdom that will never be destroyed ... . It will crush all those kingdoms and bring them to an end, but it will itself endure forever. This is the meaning of the vision of the rock cut out of a mountain, but not by human hands ..."* (2:44-45).

Daniel's explanation leaves no doubt about what is to come. The next kingdom to be established is the literal, physical kingdom of God. As explained in Chapter 8, God's kingdom will be

---

[153] Husk separated from the grain.

established when Jesus returns as King of Kings and Lord of Lords. Only those who are citizens of His spiritual kingdom now will enter the physical kingdom. That kingdom will endure forever.

Use and Misuse of Prophecy

Prophecy provides certain signposts so we can anticipate the future with confidence. Speculation about the time when a prophecy will be fulfilled, or how certain events will come about, misuses the purpose of prophecy. For example, regarding His return, Jesus said quite plainly, *"About that day or hour no one knows ..."* (Mark 13:32). Yet, despite this warning, over the years, various people have predicted the date when Jesus would return. They were, of course, proven wrong.

Prophecies about the future play two main roles in our lives. (1) Jesus said, *"I have told you now before it happens, so that when it does happen you will believe"* (John 14:29). Hence, the first role of prophecy is to strengthen our faith in the Word of God. Fulfillment of prophecy gives strong support to the reliability of the Holy Scriptures. (2) Prophecies are a window into God's purposes. But we must wait for their fulfillment. When they reach fulfillment, we will know it. Pointing to certain signs about His coming, Jesus said, *"When you see these things happening, you know that it is near, right at the door"* (Mark 13:29). Prophecies about the return of Jesus give us clues about when His return will be near. This is discussed in the next chapter.

Reject the False

Throughout the Scriptures, God has warned against the deceptions of false prophets. Along with the warnings about deception, the Scriptures also give us three main tests that must be applied to all prophets. The ones that do not pass all three tests are false prophets.

Chapter 14

1. A prophet's words and teachings must agree with the Holy Scriptures. If the teachings are not in agreement with the Scriptures, we can be certain that the prophet is not from God. Such a prophet and his teachings must be rejected. This is what the prophet Isaiah wrote:

   Consult God's instruction and the testimony of warning. If anyone does not speak according to this word, they have no light of dawn (Isaiah 8:20).

   There is simply no light in those who do not speak according to the Word of God we have in the Holy Scriptures.

2. The prophecies given by a prophet must be fulfilled—not just one or two, but all of them. These are the instructions Moses gave:

   You may say to yourselves, "How can we know when a message has not been spoken by the LORD?" If what a prophet proclaims in the name of the LORD does not take place or come true, that is a message the LORD has not spoken. That prophet has spoken presumptuously[154], so do not be alarmed (Deuteronomy 18:21-22).

3. The personal life of the prophet must be examined. The question must be asked: Does this prophet's lifestyle and works agree with the Holy Scriptures? Have his teachings resulted in love for others, or have they resulted in hatred and violence? This is what Jesus said:

   "Watch out for false prophets. They come to you in sheep's clothing, but inwardly they are ferocious wolves. By their fruit you will recognize them. Do people pick grapes from thornbushes, or figs from thistles?" (Matthew 7:15-16).

---

[154] Without God's authority.

Conclusion

Understanding of prophecies is an important aspect of the Real Faith. Fulfillment of prophecy informs us that we can trust the Bible. Fulfillment of some prophecies is still in the future. We must watch and wait for their fulfillment. God will act in His own time to fulfill those prophecies. In the meantime, the Bible gives many warnings about the deceptive messages from false prophets.

In Daniel's prophecy, the main message for today is that we are living during the final stages of this world's history. The kingdom of God will be established soon, although we do not know exactly when. To enter God's kingdom, you must be a citizen of His spiritual kingdom today.

CHAPTER 15

The Signposts

As you have read in the previous chapter, the next astounding event on the world's stage will be the return of Jesus Christ as the King of Kings and Lord of Lords. From the standpoint of our salvation, the most important prophecies given in the Bible are about the return of Jesus. You must become the citizens of His spiritual kingdom now (see Chapter 8). Without that, you will not enter His Heavenly kingdom when He comes again the second time.

From the time when Jesus returned to Heaven, His followers have wondered when this event would occur. No one knows when, and it is not wise to speculate about the time. But, the Holy Scriptures point to many signs to alert us when Jesus' coming is near.

The Olivet Prophecy

Jesus Himself laid out a roadmap pointing to His coming. It is commonly referred to as the Olivet Prophecy, because it was given on Olivet, the Mount of Olives, located across a valley east of Jerusalem.

> As Jesus was sitting on the Mount of Olives, the disciples came to him privately. "Tell us," they said, "when will this happen ... ?" (Matthew 24:3).

Jesus had just stunned the disciples a little while earlier by telling them that the temple—the pride of Jerusalem and of the Jewish people—would be destroyed. No Jew could ever think that the holy temple of God would be destroyed. But, Jesus said, *"Truly I tell you, not one stone here will be left on another; every one will be thrown down"* (24:2).

Just as Jesus had predicted, the temple was destroyed roughly 40 years after His ascension to Heaven, in 70 A.D.,[155] by the Roman armies. The prophecy is so precise that even today one can see huge hand-cut boulders, each weighing several tons, from the temple buildings that were thrown down almost 2,000 years ago. The only remaining part of the temple still standing today is the western wall that supports the large platform on which the temple, built by King Solomon, had once stood.[156]

In the minds of the disciples, if the temple was not going to exist any longer, that should be the end of the present era. Hence, the disciples had asked, *"Tell us"* ... *"when will this happen, and what will be the sign of your coming and of the end of the age?"* (24:3). But, Jesus answered, *"Watch out that no one deceives you"* (24:4). He suggested that His coming would not occur when the Roman armies surround Jerusalem and destroy the temple. Jesus then outlined what all would happen before His coming. Jesus essentially gave a scenario that would unfold in three main stages.

Stage One

> *"You will hear of wars and rumors of wars, but see to it that you are not alarmed. Such things must happen, but the end is still to come"* (Matthew 24:6).

This is the first stage—marked by the words, "the end is still to come;" the end is not yet. The world has already seen two World

---

[155] A.D. stands for Anno Domini—in the year of our Lord. It roughly means after the birth of Jesus.

[156] Today, two Muslim structures, built during the late 7th to early 8th centuries A.D., stand on this platform where the temple built by Solomon had once stood.

Wars, but this age was not supposed to end at that time. Will a third world war take place? We do not know. But, Jesus prophesied that wars would continue.

Stage Two

> "Nation will rise against nation, and kingdom against kingdom. There will be famines and earthquakes in various places. All these are the beginning of birth pains.
>
> "Then you will be handed over to be persecuted and put to death, and you will be hated by all nations because of me. At that time many will turn away from the faith and will betray and hate each other, and many false prophets will appear and deceive many people. Because of the increase in wickedness, the love of most will grow cold, but the one who stands firm to the end will be saved" (Matthew 24:7–13).

The above passage describes the second stage, marked by the words, "these are the beginning of birth pains." It is a long period, with many things happening. We just don't know how long this period will last. It is marked by both man-made and natural disasters occurring in various places around the world. Although these events have always occurred, their frequency and intensity are evident. It is a period of turmoil and suffering around the world, under demonic forces of evil. This period is marked by wickedness. The wicked people[157] will have no love for their fellow human beings, because they do not know the true God, who is love.

During this same period, the followers of Jesus are hated, persecuted, and even killed. They are persecuted because of their faith in Jesus—they hold on to the Real Faith without giving in to the forces of evil. It makes the wicked furious, who engage in religious persecution. To make it clear, Jesus also said, *"The time is coming when anyone who kills you will think they are offering a service to God. They will do such things because they have not known the*

---

[157] Evildoers.

Father or me" (John 16:2-3). The wicked followers of false gods think that they are serving God by killing the followers of Jesus. They think that they are eliminating the Real Faith through persecution.[158] It describes the fury of Satan in full action. During this period in particular, Satan *is filled with fury, because he knows that his time is short* (Revelation 12:12).

Deception by false prophets accompanies the events described here. Many followers of Jesus will turn away from the faith, because their faith is not firmly anchored on the Holy Scriptures and on the Lord Jesus Christ. Force used by the wicked will cause many to turn their backs on Jesus. *But the one who stands firm to the end will be saved* (Matthew 24:13) in the kingdom of God. In spite of all the opposition, there will be many who will stand firm no matter what. They are the ones who have had a deep relationship with Jesus Christ by living the new life (see Chapter 6). They are the ones who truly have the Real Faith.

We all need to examine ourselves whether we have the Real Faith to stand up to the evil forces that are upon us. This brings us to the third stage, the last one before the return of Jesus.

Stage Three

For the last stage of this world's history, Jesus prophesied:

> *"And this gospel of the kingdom will be preached in the whole world as a testimony to all nations, and then the end will come"* (24:14).

The phrase, "then the end will come," gives us the clue that this is the final time period. The Gospel of the kingdom has been reaching the world ever since Jesus gave the command to take the Gospel to the whole world:

> *"Go into all the world and preach the gospel to all creation. Whoever believes and is baptized will be saved,*

---

[158] This is happening in the world today, even though you don't hear about it through the news media.

but whoever does not believe will be condemned" (Mark 16:15-16).

Just before the end of this age, the Gospel will go out to the ends of the Earth with great power. Everyone around the world will have one last chance to hear the call to repentance before Jesus returns.

In a symbolic vision, the apostle John saw an *angel flying in midair, and he had the eternal gospel to proclaim to those who live on the earth—to every nation, tribe, language and people* (Revelation 14:6). An angel taking the Gospel to the world signifies that no earthly power will be able to stop the Gospel message from going forth. God will use every system of communication—radio, satellite, the Internet, and anything else that may yet be invented—to ensure that everyone on the Earth hears the Gospel of salvation.

The message of the Gospel is already going out today, but it will spread with greater speed all over the world. Despite opposition and persecution, people around the world will learn about the Real Faith.

As always, people will have the choice to accept or reject the Lord Jesus. The eternal destiny of everyone will be decided according to the choice they make.

The preaching of the Gospel always arouses the fury of Satan. Jesus warned that *those will be days of distress* (Mark 13:19) for His followers.

Final Signs

Just before the end comes, there will be frightening signs. These are the words of Jesus:

> *"There will be signs in the sun, moon and stars. On the earth, nations will be in anguish and perplexity at the roaring and tossing of the sea. People will faint from terror, apprehensive of what is coming on the world, for the heavenly bodies will be shaken. At that time they will see the Son of Man coming in a cloud with power and*

great glory. When these things begin to take place, stand up and lift up your heads, because your redemption[159] *is drawing near"* (Luke 21:25–28).

The turmoil and suffering on Earth have already been pointed out. The final signs, however, just before the Lord's return, will be supernatural signs that will make people faint from terror. There will be never-before-seen signs on Earth and in the sky. Even the best of scientists will be baffled, unable to explain what will be happening and why.

Only those who are citizens of God's kingdom will understand the true meaning of those signs. In their time of distress, they will take courage with great anticipation. It will mean freedom from the troubles of this world. At that time they will know without a doubt that Jesus is coming.

At the first sight of the glorious Heavenly procession of Jesus descending with all His holy angels, the followers of Jesus will cry out:

"Surely this is our God; we trusted in him, and he saved us. This is the LORD, we trusted in him; let us rejoice and be glad in his salvation" (Isaiah 25:9).

This is how the present era will end, and the kingdom of God will begin. The blueprint of salvation which began with the first coming of Jesus will be complete.

Conclusion

By reading this book, you have received the Gospel message. As the prophecies point out, this Earth's history is coming to a close. If you haven't made up your mind about your salvation, there is still time. But, Jesus warned, *"Look, I am coming soon!"* (Revelation 22:7). Time is slipping by.

---

[159] Freedom from sin in God's kingdom at the coming of Jesus.

CHAPTER 16

The New Age

When God's kingdom is established at the return of Jesus, this present age will have passed away. John saw a vision about the dawn of a new age: *He who was seated on the throne said, "I am making everything new!" Then he said, "Write this down, for these words are trustworthy and true"* (Revelation 21:5). The followers of Jesus will enter this new age that will never end.

This is a message of reassurance to those who keep the Real Faith till the very end. As they go through turbulent times, they will keep the faith, watching the signposts discussed in the previous chapter. For those days, the apostle reminds us: *You need to persevere ... . In just a little while, he who is coming will come and will not delay* (Hebrews 10:36-37). The apostle had absolute confidence in the return of Jesus. We must have the same confidence.

All New, Nothing Old

God assures the believers in the Real Faith that everything will be made new; nothing old will remain. John wrote:

> Then I saw *"a new heaven and a new earth,"* for the first heaven and the first earth had passed away, and there was no longer any sea. I saw the Holy City, the new Jerusalem, coming down out of heaven from God ... (Revelation 21:1-2).

This is the city that Abraham foresaw by faith. He looked forward to this city *whose architect and builder is God* (Hebrews 11:10). The believers in Jesus follow the faith of Abraham, as the apostle Paul wrote: *If you belong to Christ, then you are Abraham's seed, and heirs according to the promise* (Galatians 3:29). The promises made to Abraham will be fulfilled in the new age for all those who have put their trust in Jesus. This is what John saw in his vision:

> *And I heard a loud voice from the throne saying, "Look! God's dwelling place is now among the people, and he will dwell with them. They will be his people, and God himself will be with them and be their God.*
>
> *"He will wipe every tear from their eyes. There will be no more death or mourning or crying or pain, for the old order of things has passed away"* (Revelation 21:3-4).

No traces of the old order, the present age, will remain. In the new age, God's people will live with Jesus, the Father, and the Holy Spirit. There will be no more disease, pain, or death. The apostle Paul has referred to death as the enemy, which will be destroyed: *The last enemy to be destroyed is death* (1 Corinthians 15:26).

Who Will Be There?

As pointed out in some of the previous chapters, there are only two groups of people. We see the same thing again, at the beginning of the new age. The first group is made up of people who are victorious over sin despite the attacks of evildoers. They will inherit the Holy City, the New Jerusalem.

> *He said to me ... "Those who are victorious will inherit all this, and I will be their God and they will be my children"* (Revelation 21:6-7).

The second group will not enter the Holy City of God. Instead, they will be cast into the fiery lake of burning sulfur, which is hellfire. Their major sins are mentioned here:

Chapter 16

"But the cowardly, the unbelieving, the vile, the murderers, the sexually immoral, those who practice magic arts, the idolaters and all liars—they will be consigned to the fiery lake of burning sulfur. This is the second death" (21:8).

The cowards are those who have persecuted the innocent people of God. Based on their religious practices, they are also steeped in other sins, without shame. In fact, they are proud of their sins. The unbelieving are those who have rejected the salvation offered by Jesus.

In His justice, God must destroy sin and sinners. The hellfire is primarily *prepared for the devil and his angels* (Matthew 25:41), the first unrepentant sinners who brought sin into this world. But, to purify the universe and remove sin once and for all, the unbelievers must also be cast into hellfire. The fires of hell will end sin.

This is a warning to all that rejecting the grace and mercy of God, offered through Jesus Christ, is sin. It is disobedience to God, because He has commanded, *"You shall have no other gods before me"* (Exodus 20:2).

The Renewal

In the new age, God will renew what our first parents, Adam and Eve, lost in the Garden of Eden. The prophet John recorded what he saw:

Then the angel showed me the river of the water of life, as clear as crystal, flowing from the throne of God and of the Lamb down the middle of the great street of the city. The great street of the city was of gold, as pure as transparent glass (Revelation 22:1-2; 21:21).

On each side of the river stood the tree of life, bearing twelve crops of fruit, yielding its fruit every month. ... No longer will there be any curse (22:2-3).

The world that we live in was cursed because the first man and woman disobeyed God. No more curse in the new age suggests that there will be no more sin. Sin's consequences have been deadly, and it will not arise again.

> *The throne of God and of the Lamb will be in the city, and his servants will serve him. They will see his face, and his name will be on their foreheads. And they will reign for ever and ever* (22:3-4, 5).

The city will have the thrones of God and the Lamb, Jesus. They, along with the Holy Spirit, are One God (see Chapter 7). Notice the singular: *His servants will serve him* (22:3), referring to the One God. All the redeemed will live with God forever.

> John also wrote: "*I did not see a temple in the city, because the Lord God Almighty and the Lamb are its temple*" (21:22).

Until a few years after the ascension of Jesus, there was a temple in Jerusalem. In the New Jerusalem, however, there is no need of a temple, because God will be the temple. This signifies that the citizens of the Heavenly kingdom will continue to worship God forever.

Mirror Reflection

The picture of the new age is the best that the prophet was able to describe in human language. It is just a faint reflection of the reality to come. The apostle Paul wrote: *For now we see only a reflection as in a mirror; then we shall see face to face* (1 Corinthians 13:12).

The reality will be much more glorious than what we can now imagine. Yes, it may sound outlandish to some, but in His kingdom we will see God face to face. The apostle wrote: *What no eye has seen, what no ear has heard, and what no human mind has conceived—the things God has prepared for those who love him— these are the things God has revealed to us by his Spirit* (1 Corinthians 2:9-10).

Chapter 16

Conclusion

With this chapter the message of this book comes to a close. You need to ask yourself only one question: "Will I enter the Holy City when the new age begins, or will I be in the fiery lake of burning sulfur?" Those are the two destinies. There is nothing in between or outside those two. Only Jesus can help you prepare so you can enter the Holy City. If you commit your life to Him, He will keep the gate of that city wide open for you to enter. Amen.

Postscript

I trust that the message of this book has helped you spiritually. If so, I would like to hear from you. You can write to me by filling out the contact form at the publisher's website:

www.elinapub.com

Give your family, friends, neighbors, and even strangers a clear understanding of salvation and eternal life. You may never know what rewards your gift will bring until you are welcomed into the Heavenly kingdom. May you hear from the Master these words:

> "Well done, good and faithful servant! You have been faithful with a few things; I will put you in charge of many things. Come and share your master's happiness!" (Matthew 25:21).

Order extra copies from: amazon.com, elinapub.com, or other retail outlets.

If I don't get to meet you in this world, I hope to meet you in the Heavenly kingdom. So, I close by saying to you,

> "The LORD bless you and keep you;
>
> the LORD make his face shine on you
> and be gracious to you;
>
> the LORD turn his face toward you
> and give you peace" (Numbers 6:24–26).
> Amen.

D. A. Singh

APPENDIX I

Glossary

Amen: Saying this word indicates that you agree. In the New Testament, it is also a title of Jesus.

Angel: A heavenly being sent out from God's throne.

Apostle: Someone who was sent out to take Jesus' teachings to others. Some of the apostles, such as Paul, Peter, and John, were also prophets. God used them to write portions of the Holy Scriptures and to predict future events.

Aramaic: The common language spoken in Jesus' day.

Archeology: Study of ancient people and events from evidence found through systematic diggings on ancient sites.

Ascension: The return of Jesus to Heaven, as He was lifted up in the presence of His followers.

Atonement: Forgiveness and removal of sin by Jesus.

Atoning sacrifice: Jesus' sacrifice that brings forgiveness of sins and makes it possible for us to come to God.

B.C.: Before Christ.

Believer: A person who has made a commitment to follow Jesus.

Blasphemy: Speaking evil of God, or taking the place of God.

Born again: Also referred to as being born of God. The experience of conversion after repentance and acceptance of Jesus' sacrifice on the cross for our sins.

Centurion: An officer in charge of 100 soldiers in the Roman army.

Christ: Jesus, who was the Messiah—the one who came to deliver humanity from sin.

Church: An assembly of people who are followers of Jesus.

Commandments: Rules of living that God has given to us.

Condemnation: Punishment after a person is found guilty in a judgment.

Confess: Own up your sins before God.

Contrite: Feeling sorry and remorseful before God.

Deity (Godhead): The One God who can be described as a family of three beings who have always existed and will always exist in perfect unity.

Disciple: Close follower of Jesus.

Divine: Of the same nature as God.

End of the age: A time when the present era will come to an end. The last stage of this earth's history.

Eternal life: Life without death. Living forever with God.

Eyewitness: Someone who has seen certain things and events with his/her own eyes.

Fury: Fierce anger.

Gentile: Non-Jew.

Godhead (Deity): The One God who can be described as a family of three beings who have always existed and will always exist in perfect unity.

Gospel: The message of salvation through the grace of Jesus Christ.

Grace: What God does for humans out of His goodness and lovingkindness. God forgives our sins by His grace, something we did not deserve.

Holy people: Those who believe in Christ and live a life of victory over sin.

Jews: Descendants of Abraham and those who have converted to Judaism from some other religion. They accept the Old Testament, but do not believe in Jesus as the Savior.

Jordan: The main river in Israel.

Kingdom of God: Also called, "kingdom of Heaven" and "kingdom of light." Jesus Himself represents the kingdom of God. The

Glossary

believers in Jesus—those who have been born again—are citizens of the kingdom of God now. They will inherit the physical kingdom when Jesus returns to this earth a second time.

Lamb: In the Holy Scriptures, the lamb is used as a symbol for Jesus as the Sinless One who carried the sins of the world and was slaughtered (crucified) as a sacrifice.

Mantras: Repetitious verbal formulas, generally in a language that is not commonly used, that people use in an effort to find forgiveness and salvation.

Manuscript: A book written by hand.

Mercy: God's love and kindness.

Messiah: Christ (Jesus). It was commonly known among the Jewish people that the Messiah would be the Son of God, and would be from the line of King David.

Missionary: One who is sent out to share the message of Jesus with others.

Pagans: People who do not believe in the one true God found in the Holy Scriptures.

Parable: A story that teaches a spiritual lesson.

Perish: To die under the condemnation of sin, and without any hope of salvation.

Persecute: To bully and mistreat the followers of Jesus.

Persecution: Mistreatment of the followers of Jesus by unbelievers.

Pharisee: Pharisees belonged to a religious sect in the time of Jesus. Members of this sect thought that they had salvation because they were religious.

Prophecy: A message from God that may also include future events told before they happen, under Heavenly guidance.

Prophet: Someone who brings a message from God and also tells the future under God's guidance.

Reconciled: Accepted by God and united with Him.

Redeem (verb): God's action of forgiveness and deliverance from sin for those who accept the sacrifice of Jesus on the cross.

Redeemed (noun): Those who are forgiven and delivered from sin by accepting the sacrifice of Jesus on the cross.

Redemption: (1) Forgiveness and deliverance from sin accomplished by Jesus for all those who believe in Him. (2) Freedom from sin in God's kingdom at the coming of Jesus.

Reign: Rule.

Repent: To confess your sins to God, and turn away from past sinful ways.

Repentance: Confession of sins to God with humility, and turning away from past sinful ways.

Resurrection: Becoming alive after being dead.

Revelation: Something that is made known.

Righteous (persons): Those who have repented of their sins and accepted Jesus, and live in obedience to His commands.

Righteousness: God's holiness.

Saints: Those who believe in Christ and live a life of victory over sin.

Salvation: Freedom from the condemnation of sin, and the assurance of God's gift of eternal life.

Sanctify: Make pure.

Sanhedrin: The ancient Jewish supreme council or religious court in Jerusalem.

Scepter: The king's royal baton that indicated his authority as the ruler.

Son of God: Jesus, who was God, came in the form of a man, as the Messiah, and had no human father.

Son of Man: Jesus often identified Himself with humanity by referring to Himself as the Son of Man.

Synagogue: Jewish place of worship and assembly.

Tithe: One-tenth.

Transgression: Sin. Disobedience of God's commandments.

Unbeliever: Someone who rejects the Gospel of Jesus Christ.

Unrighteousness: Sinfulness.

Wicked: Evildoer.

Wickedness: Evildoing.

APPENDIX II

Books of the Holy Scriptures

Note: The books cited in this work are highlighted.

39 Books of the Old Testament

Genesis	Ezra	Joel
Exodus	Nehemiah	**Amos**
Leviticus	**Esther**	Obadiah
Numbers	Job	Jonah
Deuteronomy	**Psalms**	**Micah**
Joshua	Proverbs	**Nahum**
Judges	**Ecclesiastes**	Habakkuk
Ruth	Song of Songs	Zephaniah
1 Samuel	**Isaiah**	Haggai
2 Samuel	**Jeremiah**	**Zechariah**
1 Kings	Lamentations	**Malachi**
2 Kings	Ezekiel	
1 Chronicles	**Daniel**	
2 Chronicles	**Hosea**	

27 Books of the New Testament

Matthew	**Ephesians**	**Hebrews**
Mark	**Philippians**	**James**
Luke	**Colossians**	**1 Peter**
John	**1 Thessalonians**	**2 Peter**
Acts	**2 Thessalonians**	**1 John**
Romans	**1 Timothy**	2 John
1 Corinthians	**2 Timothy**	3 John
2 Corinthians	Titus	Jude
Galatians	Philemon	**Revelation**

Index

Abraham's faith. *See* faith
Babylon
   call to come out of, 126
   confusion, 125
baptism, 60
   a holy rite, 61
   commitment to God, 61
believe
   four things, 58
born again. *See* born anew
born anew, 62
   a child of God, 64
   everyone must be, 62
   how to be, 62
   through a simple prayer, 64
choice
   everyone must make, 131
   two foundations, 133
   two gates, 131
   two kingdoms, 135
   two roads, 131
cross, the
   finished the need for sacrifices, 54
   for all people, 38
   meaning of, 36
   the finished work, 38
   was God's purpose, 37
Deity. *See* God
devil. *See* enemy
devotional life, 66
enemy, the
   a cherub who sinned, 118
   expelled from heaven, 115
   facts about, 117-118
   has been condemned, 135
   his end, 123
   Jesus overcame, 127

enemy, the (*Continued*)
   Lucifer became the devil, 122
   Satan, 122
eternal life
   for whoever believes, 21
   Jesus gives, 23
   through forgiveness of sins, 22
evil
   how it began, 116
   keep away from, 124
evil one. *See* enemy
faith. *See* also Real Faith
   Abraham's, 147, 148
   Abraham's faith in Jesus, 149
   and obedience, 146
   confidence about things not seen, 146
   looks forward to a heavenly city, 147
   makes us grow spiritually, 150
   many will turn away from, 179
fasting, 71
   Jesus' teaching on, 72
fellowship, 74
forgiveness
   brings eternal life, 22
   by grace, not by works, 65
   must repent to receive, 58-59
   the greatest need, 7
God
   born of, 62

Index

God (*Continued*)
  can be known only through Jesus, 78
  consuming fire, 27
  Deity, 15, 88
  His word will not return empty, 154
  in the person of Jesus Christ, 27
  is love, 25, 27, 179
  made peace with us, 27
  meaning of One God, 14-15, 88
  more loving than any human parent, 24
  no other God, 15, 78
  perfect unity, 15
  submit to, 128
  waiting with open arms, 24

God's
  grace, 8
  love, 21, 25, 26
  mercy, 8

Godhead. *See* God

Gospel, the
  advice on sharing, 84
  arouses Satan's fury, 181
  four types of responses, 99-100
  power of God, 84
  what it is, 83-84

grace
  sins forgiven by God's, 9

hellfire
  for devil and his angels, 185
  will end sin, 185

Holy Scriptures, the
  a wonder, 157
  accusations of change are baseless, 163
  are a complete set, 159
  authors, 158
  confidence in, 160, 163, 168
  given by the Holy Spirit, 158
  God speaks through, 63

Holy Scriptures (*Continued*)
  God's will found in, 69
  God's word, 154
  have stood all tests, 155
  purpose of, 160-161
  rebuke sin, 166
  reliability of, 163
  to test other writings and teachings, 165, 175
  understanding of, 161
  uniqueness of, 153, 157, 163

Holy Spirit, 87
  agent that gave the Scriptures, 158
  receiving, 91
  role in salvation, 89
  the divine helper, 90
  the One name includes, 89
  who is?, 88
  work of (in our lives), 92-93

Jesus
  alive for ever, 40
  before Abraham, 13-14, 163
  born to be the Son, 17
  came because we could not approach God, 24
  came to save sinners, 20
  came for the entire human race, 19
  carried our sins, 35
  eyewitnesses to His glory, 18
  forgave sin, 9, 20-21
  fullness of the Godhead, 15
  God with us, 16
  High Priest in heaven, 54
  His second coming, 109-110
  Isaiah's prophecy, 16
  King of Kings, Lord of Lords, 96
  looking for you, 23
  only way to God's throne, 16
  open the door to, 60
  opened the way to God, 10
  overcame Satan, 127-128

Index

Jesus (*Continued*)
- represented kingdom of God, 96
- resurrection and the life, 44
- resurrection of. *See* resurrection
- return to heaven, 53
- salvation in no one else, 19, 21, 38
- Son of Man, 21
- the Father's voice, 18, 89
- the One who saves, 19, 124
- the Word, 13
- tomb, empty, 44
- tomb, sealed and guarded, 42
- transfiguration of, 18
- unique person in history, 105
- was sinless, 36
- who is?, 13
- why the cross?, 27
- why the cry, My God, My God . . ., 35
- why the only way, 37
- will come back, 53, 106
- Yeshua (in Hebrew), 19

kingdom of God
- and repentance, 95
- continues to grow, 98
- example of mustard seed, 97
- followers of Jesus are in, 97
- future heavenly kingdom, 100-101
- Jesus' followers will rule with Him, 103
- Jesus represented, 96
- not everyone will enter, 138
- ruled by Jesus, 101, 102
- some will never be citizens, 99
- two groups: sheep and goats, 101
- will never end, 137

kingdom of heaven. *See* kingdom of God

Lucifer. *See* enemy

need
- Hezekiah's, 5
- Peter's, 6
- the greatest, 7
- what it is, 5

new age, the
- all made new, 183
- no more sin, 186
- no traces of old, 184
- who will be there?, 184

new believer, 67

new life
- in harmony with God's will, 65

peace
- inner, 85
- with others, 85

persecution
- because of faith in Jesus, 179
- Gospel will spread despite, 181
- of Jesus' followers, 125
- Satan's fury, 180

praise, 73

pray
- for salvation of others, 69
- how not to, 67

prayer, 67
- come to the throne of God in, 68, 92
- do not lose heart, 71
- in the name of Jesus, 67-68
- no special words for, 67
- of repentance, 64
- present requests to God in, 67
- the Holy Spirit helps in, 92
- the Lord's, 68
- true prayer, 67

prophecy
- about crucifixion, 32
- about Cyrus, 171

prophecy (*Continued*)
  about destruction of the temple, 178
  about division of Jesus' clothes, 144-145
  about future events, 172-173, 178-182
  about how blood money was used, 144
  about Jesus' birth, 142-143
  about Jesus' silence during trial, 31
  about Judas the betrayer, 144
  about resurrection of Jesus, 55-56, 145
  about return of Jesus, 53, 106
  about rise and fall of empires, 169-172
  about who Jesus is, 16
  God with us, 16
  its use and misuse, 174
  news in advance, 168
  on the cross, offer of vinegar, 35
  pierced for our sins, 37
  serves two main purposes, 168
  the author of, 167
prophets, false
  tests to apply, 175
Real Faith, the
  accepting the sacrifice of Jesus, 39
  and Holy Scriptures, 3
  based on evidence, 145
  begins like a tiny seed, 141
  begins with belief in Jesus, 24
  different in two major ways, 142
  faith in the one and only savior, 54
  firmly based on the resurrection, 53

Real Faith, the (*Continued*)
  lifelong journey with Christ, 65
  must grow and bear fruit, 141
  needs met through, 5, 7
  of Abraham, 148
  requires obedience to God, 75
  sharing, 83
  the Holy Spirit helps us grow in, 91-93
  through the cross, 38
  trust in God, 73
repent
  how to, 59-60
  turn around, change, 60
repentance
  and kingdom of God, 57, 95
  attitude of a child, 61
  prayer of, 64
  salvation cannot be obtained without, 59
resurrection
  among the disciples, 49-50
  breakfast with disciples, 51
  meaning of Jesus', 52
  of believers at the return of Jesus, 113
  power to rise, 43
  reason for faith, 53
  the empty tomb, 44
  the open tomb, 43
  the risen Lord, 45-47
  the vision of Saul, 51-52
return of Jesus. *See* second coming of Jesus
salvation
  assurance of, 70, 92, 106
  blueprint of, 106
  citizenship in God's kingdom, 95
  Jesus is able to save completely, 54
  one day it will be too late, 63, 136

Index

salvation (*Continued*)
  reason why it is found in no one else, 128
  received by faith in Jesus, 65, 161
  the blood of Jesus guarantees, 84
Satan. *See* enemy
second coming of Jesus
  a great multitude will greet Him, 112
  events on earth, 178-180
  final signs, 181
  His sign in the sky, 111
  joy for the followers of Jesus, 111-112
  many will mourn, 110
  resurrection of believers, 113
  six main points about, 107-108
  the last stage, 180
  to judge the world, 108-109
  what it will be like, 109-110
sin
  beginning of, 117
  confess, 59
  end of, 185-186
  example of Gehazi, 82-83

sin (*Continued*)
  God blots out, 69
  how entered the world, 121
  is disobeying God, 7, 75, 121
  knowledge through God's law, 77
  must be punished, 27, 37
  no one is without, 7, 22
  no worse than another, 81
  offends God, 27, 35
  rebellion against God, 119
  separates from God, 35, 121
  some may only appear small, 81
  wages of, 57
  when we stumble and fall, 76
  who's responsible?, 121
Ten Commandments, the
  summary of, 77-80
  written by God, 77
thanksgiving, 72
tithe, 100
trials
  allowed to build faith, 70
  brought by the evil one, 70
Word, the
  became flesh, 14, 16

NOTES

www.ingramcontent.com/pod-product-compliance
Lightning Source LLC
Chambersburg PA
CBHW071456040426
42444CB00008B/1358